Reflections

Reflections

God's Good News in the Miracles of Jesus

Roger Ellsworth

DayOne

© Day One Publications 2013
First Edition 2013

Unless otherwise indicated, Scripture quotations are from the New King
James Version (NKJV)®. Copyright © 1982 by Thomas Nelson, Inc. Used by
permission. All rights reserved.

British Library Cataloguing in Publication Data available

ISBN 978-1-84625-407-9

Published by Day One Publications
Ryelands Road, Leominster, HR6 8NZ

☎ 01568 613 740
FAX: 01568 611 473
email—sales@dayone.co.uk
web site—www.dayone.co.uk
North American e-mail—usasales@dayone.co.uk
North American web site—www.dayonebookstore.com

Designed by Wayne McMaster
Printed and bound by TJ International Ltd, Padstow Cornwall

Dedicated to the Friday-nighters:
Calee Clark
Rebecca Evans
Luke Ferguson
Amelia Krauss
Tucker Messamore
Will Miller
Josh Morgan
Michael O'Malley

Commendations

This is typical Roger Ellsworth: simple and accurate, pointed and practical, warm and Christ-centred. Further, and very important in a work on Christ's miracles, here are no foolish natural 'explanations', but rather Bible-honouring expositions.

John Legg, retired pastor with itinerant preaching ministry in South Wales

In today's 'miracle' theology, much is made of self-manufactured biblical content. Everything seems to be a miracle of sorts, which in turn renders miracles mundane, if not altogether useless. If miracles are to be true in the biblical sense of the word, they are not in anyway the norm.

What Roger Ellsworth does is to bring us back to earth concerning the miracles. As he states, 'Miracles can be defined as deeds that take us out of the realm of the ordinary into the realm of the extraordinary.'

If everything is a miracle, as so many embrace in our day of extra-biblical revelation, there is no necessity for miracles. As has been stated by many biblical scholars, miracles must be interventions, not movements that continually provide the providential elements of God's decrees.

If you want to come back to earth regarding miracle overkill, read this book. It will set your feet on solid ground without the grandstanding of perpetual implication of the miraculous in every event.

Dr Ellsworth is a man of character and an outstanding expositor of Scripture. He knows well that miracles are not preeminent to God's designed providential execution of his ordained affairs, which does in fact encompass miracles, but not to the extremity that so many have embraced in our day of sensationalism. The fact is that Ellsworth is primarily lifting up the glory of Christ, not the miracles. He knows well that Christ is the Standard-bearer of his own creation.

It is my opinion that you will certainly come back again and again to Dr Ellsworth's precision in doctrine.

Roy Hargrave, Pastor, Riverbend Community Church, Ormond Beach, Florida, USA

Contents

7

Acknowledgements

My warmest thanks go to Jim Holmes for allowing me the privilege of publishing with Day One. I am also grateful for the expert help of Suzanne Mitchell in the editing process. As always, I have been blessed by the valuable assistance of my wife, Sylvia. I am thankful for her and for her help.

Introduction

Jesus of Nazareth, a Man attested by God to you by miracles, wonders, and signs which God did through Him in your midst …

Acts 2:22

There are four types of miracles in the Bible: those performed by God in the Old Testament era (e.g., the burning bush, the parting of the Red Sea, the protection of the three men who were cast into a furnace); those performed by Jesus; those performed by the apostles; and those performed through Satanic power.

The following chapters are about the miracles of Jesus. No one can read much of any of the four Gospels without soon encountering a miracle that Jesus performed, and no one can consider him- or herself to be a student of Scripture without deeply pondering these miracles.

What are miracles?

Miracles can be defined as deeds that take us out of the realm of the ordinary into the realm of the extraordinary. We can also put it this way: miracles are powerful deeds in the physical realm that illustrate and reveal profound truths about the spiritual realm.

Think about this physical realm. When God created it, he put in place some natural laws to govern and control it. A miracle occurs when God temporarily suspends the natural laws to do something of an extraordinary nature in the physical realm. It is God breaking into the natural order to do something supernatural.

It should go without saying, then, that anything that happens regularly and frequently is not a miracle. We sometimes hear people refer to 'the miracle of childbirth'. But childbirth is not a miracle. It is in keeping with natural laws that God set in place. It has been estimated that well over sixty billion people have been born on earth. Something that has happened that frequently cannot be classified as a miracle!

Some Christians assume that miracles happened almost every day in the period of time covered by Scripture, and they insist that we should be seeing miracles on a daily basis today. It is difficult to understand how something that occurs on a daily basis can be considered a miracle. In addition to that, we must note that miracles did not happen all that frequently in Scripture. They were rather confined to four periods that were separated by centuries:

- The period during which the people of Israel were delivered from Egypt and established in the land of Canaan;
- The period during which the prophets Elijah and Elisha were involved in the life-and-death struggle against false religion;
- The period during which God's people were in captivity in Babylon;

• The period during which the Lord Jesus Christ and his apostles ministered.

Taken together, these periods comprise a very small part of the great number of years covered by Scripture.

How can we be sure that Jesus performed the miracles reported by the Gospels?

Many have little regard for Jesus. They consider him to have been a mere man. Some even think that he was a very bad man. They view him as one who hoodwinked people into thinking that he was someone special.

Such people dismiss the miracles of Jesus. They think that these things never happened and that his disciples just made up the stories.

But the miracles of Jesus are stubborn things. As we read the Gospel accounts, we note three features about them:

• They were great in number: Jesus did not perform only a few of them;
• They were varied in character: he did not perform only one kind;
• They were witnessed by many: he did not perform them in secret.

To put it another way, if Jesus only performed in secret one kind of miracle on only one or two occasions, we would do well to be suspicious and doubtful. But that is not what the Gospels report.

Why did Jesus do miracles?

TO PROVE HIS IDENTITY

It should not surprise us to find the era of Jesus on the above list of periods during which miracles occurred. The verse from Acts cited at the start of this Introduction shows us that Jesus's miracles were designed to validate or prove that he was God in human flesh. While imprisoned, John the Baptist had a bout with doubt as to whether Jesus was indeed the Messiah. John sent two of his disciples to ask Jesus this question: 'Are You the Coming One, or do we look for another?' (Matt. 11:3). Jesus answered with these words: 'Go and tell John the things which you hear and see: The blind see and the lame walk; the lepers are cleansed and the deaf hear; the dead are raised up and the poor have the gospel preached to them. And blessed is he who is not offended because of Me' (11:4–6). John the Baptist wanted to know if Jesus was indeed God in human flesh, and Jesus answered by pointing him to the miracles. Those miracles proved his identity.

The Lord Jesus also appealed to his miracles when the religious leaders of Jerusalem wanted to stone him for claiming to be God. Jesus said to them: 'If I do not do the works of My Father, do not believe Me; but if I do, though you do not believe Me, believe the works, that you may know and believe that the Father is in Me, and I in Him' (John 10:37–38).

In explaining the writing of his Gospel, the apostle John tells us that he selected a few of the many miracles Jesus did so that his readers 'may believe that Jesus is the Christ, the Son

* POOR IN SPIRIT

of God' and that in believing they 'may have life in His name' (John 20:31).

To understand the miracles of Jesus, we need to understand Jesus himself. Out of all the billions of people who have lived, Jesus was unique. He was the God-Man: he was fully God and fully man at one and the same time. Paul puts it succinctly: 'God was in Christ' (2 Cor. 5:19). The miracles of Jesus prove that assertion.

TO PICTURE HIS WORK

If we say that Jesus's miracles were critical elements in revealing him to be the Son of God, we have spoken the truth, but we have not yet said enough about those miracles. We must connect them with Jesus's purpose for being on this earth. Why did he come? The angel who announced his impending birth to Joseph said, '… you shall call His name JESUS, for He will save His people from their sins' (Matt. 1:21).

Jesus himself stated his mission on more than one occasion. In Mark 10:45, he affirmed that he had come to 'give His life a ransom for many'. On another occasion, he said he had come 'to seek and to save that which was lost' (Luke 19:10).

Jesus was here, then, on a saving mission. He was here to provide the basis on which God the Father could forgive sinners their sins and give them a right standing with himself. He was here to rescue sinners from the condemnation of hell and to make them citizens of heaven.

By living in perfect obedience to his Father's holy law, Jesus provided the righteousness that God demands of each of us. By dying on the cross, Jesus received the penalty for our unrighteous living. He actually received on that cross an eternity's worth of wrath for all who receive him as their Lord and Saviour.

Sinners are saved—delivered from their sins—when the Holy Spirit of God applies the saving work of Christ to them. This application constitutes a radical change. The saving work of Christ will also mean a radical change one day for the created order that has been ravaged by man's sin.

The miracles of Jesus are pictures of all these things. The miracles by means of which he delivered suffering individuals picture in the physical realm the nature of the spiritual salvation he came to provide. The miracles by which he demonstrated his authority over nature picture that glorious day when creation will be finally freed from the devastating effects of man's sin. (For further development of these pictures, see the last chapter.)

So in his miracles, Christians find both the truth about Jesus and the truth about his saving work on their behalf. The truths we find should set our hearts singing. The Christ who did mighty deeds in the physical realm during his public ministry has done mighty deeds for us in the spiritual realm, and will do more mighty deeds in the future. So we join in the psalmist's exultation: 'The LORD has done great things for us, and we are glad' (Ps. 126:3).

A glimpse
of his glory
(John 2:1–11)

On the third day there was a wedding in Cana of Galilee, and the mother of Jesus was there. Now both Jesus and His disciples were invited to the wedding. And when they ran out of wine, the mother of Jesus said to Him, 'They have no wine.'

John 2:1–3

The changing of water into wine is the first of eight miracles that the apostle John reports from the public ministry of Jesus (the others are recorded in 4:46–54; 5:1–9; 6:5–13; 6:19–21; 9:1–7; 11:1–44; 21:1–11). This miracle was performed in Cana. John states that this was a town in Galilee, but its precise location is unknown today. The timing of this miracle was 'the third day' (v. 1)—that is, the third day after Jesus called Philip and Nathanael to be his disciples (1:43–51).[1]

Why did Jesus attend the wedding in Cana? Some have suggested that he merely wanted to show that he could enter into life's joyful occasions and that he was not a prudish killjoy. Others have offered the view that Jesus wanted to set his stamp of approval on marriage. Still others say that Jesus wanted to show his concern for even the small details of life.

While containing some validity, these explanations do not give due weight to John's explanation for Jesus's presence in Cana: that is, to manifest his glory and, in so doing, to cause his believing disciples to believe even more (v. 11). We must focus on John's explanation and not allow ourselves to be sidetracked by the above suggestions.

Jesus manifested the glory of his person

Jesus and his disciples had been invited to attend a wedding. Wine, a symbol of joy (Judg. 9:13; Ps. 104:15; Eccles. 10:19), was considered essential for such a joyous occasion. It was no small thing, therefore, when the wine ran out (v. 3). Such a calamity could even have been viewed as an ill-omen for the young couple.

Mary knew what to do on this occasion. She reported the situation to Jesus in these simple words: 'They have no wine.'

Jesus responded in this way: 'Woman, what does your concern have to do with Me? My hour has not yet come' (v. 4).

Jesus's answer has caused some to think that he was rude to his mother. In reality, he was being very kind to her. Anthony T. Selvaggio notes that Jesus's question, 'What does your concern have to do with Me?', could equally well be translated 'What do you and I have in common?' Selvaggio then writes of Jesus,

> He was reminding His mother that though He was her son, He was ultimately her Lord. That is why He asked, 'What do you and I have in common?' On one level Mary and Jesus had much in common, but at another level they were worlds apart. He was the eternal Son of God, and she was just another sinful descendant of Adam.[2]

When the Lord reveals to any of us the gap between himself and us and our desperate need of him, he is being kind—very kind—to us.

Jesus was sufficient for the crisis. He commanded that six water pots be filled with water (v. 7). Then he said, 'Draw some out now, and take it to the master of the feast' (v. 8). When the master tasted it, he recognized it as wine.

This miracle proved that Jesus was no ordinary man but was, as John has already testified, filled with the glory of the 'only begotten' of the Father (1:18). J. C. Ryle writes of Jesus, 'After thirty years' seclusion at Nazareth, He now for the first time lifted up the veil which He had thrown over His divinity in becoming flesh, and revealed something of His almighty power and Godhead.'[3]

This miracle was a fitting way for Jesus to begin his public ministry. Wine, sometimes associated with abundance, illustrated Jesus entering his ministry in an abundant way. The glory he showed at Cana was the harbinger of the 'greater things' to come that Jesus had promised (1:50).

Jesus manifested the glory of his salvation

In this miracle, Jesus manifested his power not merely to change one thing into another, but to change it into something radically different and far superior.

We cannot ponder Jesus's power to change without thinking of salvation. There is no more radical change, and it comes about only through him.

By referring to his 'hour' (v. 4), Jesus himself plainly indicated that he intended his action at Cana to point towards the saving work he came to this earth to perform. The apostle John emphatically declares that the hour to which Jesus referred was his death on the cross (7:6, 8, 30; 8:20; 12:23; 13:1). Why was it necessary for Jesus to die on the cross? To provide salvation for sinners!

So Jesus wanted his miracle to be interpreted in light of his coming death, a death through which he would purchase salvation for sinners. We do not interpret this miracle correctly, then, if we do not connect it to that to which Jesus himself wanted it to be connected: the salvation of sinners.

Salvation is so glorious that our minds cannot capture it nor our tongues convey it. It is glorious in the gap it spans, lifting the sinner from guilt to glory, from foulness to forgiveness, from vileness to victory, from hell to heaven, from ruin to righteousness and from judgement to justification.

It is glorious because it is the work of the glorious God. It is glorious in its demonstration that such a God could love such unworthy, undeserving sinners; that God loved those sinners without forfeiting his justice; and that God's wisdom was sufficient to satisfy the demands of both his justice and his grace.

Jesus demonstrated something of the glorious nature of salvation by using the six water pots that were there. These pots were used for the ceremonial cleansings required by Judaism (v. 6). The fact that Jesus transformed the water in these pots indicated that what he had come to do would surpass Judaism just as wine surpasses water. The Law of Moses, which was the centrepiece of Judaism, was not given by God for the purpose of bringing salvation; it was rather given so that the Jews would become keenly conscious of how impossible it was for them to attain salvation by their own efforts and in order to drive them to look forward in faith to the coming Christ. The fact that Christ was there in Cana and would soon go to the cross meant that the purpose for which the law had been given was completely fulfilled.

The miracle Jesus performed in Cana was not intended for entertainment. It was designed to cause Mary, John and the others to look back at it from the vantage point of the cross and say, 'Just as he changed water into wine, so, by his death on the cross, he changed sinners into saints.'

Mary said of the people at the feast, 'They have no wine.' There was a point at which it could be said of all believers, 'They have no life.' But the power of Jesus that changed water into wine changed our deadness into life (2 Cor. 5:17; Eph. 2:1–10). Warren Wiersbe says,

> I am reminded of the story of the drunken coal miner who was converted and became a vocal witness for Christ. One of his friends tried to trap him by asking: 'Do you believe that Jesus turned water into wine?' 'I certainly do!' the believer replied. 'In my home, He has turned wine into furniture, decent clothes, and food for my children!'[4]

Once we see the glorious nature of salvation, we cannot help but join David in saying,

> What shall I render to the LORD for all His benefits toward me?

> I will take up the cup of salvation,
>
> And call upon the name of the Lord.

(Ps. 116:12–13)

In David's day, it was customary for worshippers at the great festivals in Jerusalem to drink a cup of wine as a special expression of thanksgiving to the Lord for his blessings. Those who by God's grace have drunk from the cup of his salvation will be deeply grateful to him. The greater our understanding of our salvation, the greater our thanksgiving will be.

Jesus prefigured the glory of glory

When the master of the feast tasted the wine, he essentially said to the bridegroom, 'You have saved the best for last!'

While salvation offers many benefits and blessings in this world, these things cannot begin to compare with the glory that awaits believers in heaven (Rom. 8:18; 2 Cor. 4:16–18). J. C. Ryle notes,

> A greater marriage feast than that of Cana will one day be held, when Christ Himself will be the bridegroom and believers will be the bride. A greater glory will one day be manifested, when Jesus shall take to Himself His great power and reign. Blessed will they be in that day who are called to the marriage supper of the Lamb![5]

Only those who drink the cup of Christ's salvation in this life will be allowed to share in the marriage supper of the Lamb (Rev. 19:7–9). Those who refuse to drink from that cup of salvation now will drink from another cup in eternity—the cup of the wrath of God. Nowhere is this stated more forcefully and fearfully than in the words the angel spoke to the apostle John:

> If anyone worships the beast and his image, and receives his mark on his forehead or on his hand, he himself shall also drink of the wine of the wrath of God, which is poured out full strength into the cup of His indignation. He shall be tormented with fire and brimstone in the presence of the holy angels and in the presence of the Lamb.
>
> (Rev. 14:9–10)

Reflect on these points

1. Jesus went to Cana to manifest his glory and, in so doing, to cause his believing disciples to believe even more.

2. When the Lord reveals to any of us the gap between himself and us and our desperate need of him, he is being kind—very kind—to us.

3. Jesus wanted his miracle to be interpreted in the light of his coming death, a death through which he would purchase salvation for sinners.

4. Only those who drink the cup of Christ's salvation in this life will be allowed to share in the marriage supper of the Lamb.

A wonder
from afar
(John 4:46–54)

... There was a certain nobleman whose son was sick at Capernaum. When he heard that Jesus had come out of Judea into Galilee, he went to Him and implored Him to come down and heal his son, for he was at the point of death ... Jesus said to him, 'Go your way; your son lives.' So the man believed the word that Jesus spoke to him, and he went his way.

John 4:46–50

These verses report Jesus's healing of the son of 'a certain nobleman' (v. 46). This man was some sort of royal official. He may very well have been a Jewish man who worked in some capacity for the Roman government. The great commentator William Hendriksen suggests that he was a courtier for the tetrarch Herod Antipas.[1]

No station in life exempts us from life's harsh realities. The nobleman knew this very well. His son was critically ill, so much so that he was 'at the point of death' (v. 47).

The nobleman knew about the miracle-working power of Jesus. He had probably heard about Jesus changing the water into wine at Cana, and he may have heard about Jesus's other miracles as well. (John's remark about this healing being 'the second sign Jesus did'—v. 54—should not be taken to mean that he had done no other miracles since changing the water into wine. John 2:23 affirms that Jesus did several other miracles prior to this particular one (see also John 3:2; 4:45). Therefore, we should understand John's reference to the 'second sign' to mean that it was the second miracle Jesus did in Cana of Galilee.)

This official, who lived in Capernaum, had made his frantic journey to Cana, found Jesus and was now imploring Jesus 'to come down and heal his son' (v.47). He was correctly assuming that Jesus could help his son, but incorrectly assuming that Jesus had to be where his son was and had to get there before his son died. John's account shows us that Jesus did not have to be on the scene to heal the young man, and, as we shall see from other miracles, Jesus could both heal the sick and raise the dead.

As with all the other miracles, this miracle puts the spotlight squarely on Jesus. Yes, we commend the nobleman for coming to Jesus and for pleading so urgently and desperately for the life of his son, but he is not the hero of this story: Jesus is.

The discerning Christ (vv. 47–48)

Our hearts are touched by this story. Here is the poor, heartbroken father begging Jesus to hurry to Capernaum. We might expect to read that Jesus responded by saying, 'Yes, by all means, let's go at once!' However, Jesus said something quite different: 'Unless you people see signs and wonders, you will by no means believe' (v. 48). Jesus had lots of people in mind, and the nobleman was definitely in that group.

Why did Jesus reprimand a man who was legitimately concerned about the life of his son? The reason is that Jesus wanted the man and others to know that while he was concerned about life in this world, he was not exclusively concerned with it. The nobleman was interested only in Jesus fixing a problem in this life, and Jesus, who discerns everything, discerned this and confronted the man with it.

The nobleman is an early representative of multitudes today who are not interested in God as God but rather in God as 'the fixer'. They are not interested in the Giver but only in his gifts. Dale Ralph Davis observes that the church is in trouble when she stops saying of God, 'Thou art worthy' and begins saying to him, 'Thou art useful'.[2] Anthony Selvaggio offers this assessment: 'Evangelicalism is obsessed with pragmatism. People are seeking a God who works for them. Many in the church want a God who is both user- and seeker-friendly.'[3] David Wells says, 'We have turned to a God that we can use rather than to a God we must obey; we have turned to a God who will fulfill our needs rather than to a God before whom we must surrender our rights.'[4]

The Lord Jesus is interested in producing true faith, and this requires him to challenge and destroy false faith. True faith must have the right object—Jesus as the Saviour from sin. If it is faith in another kind of Jesus, it is a false faith. John Owen, one of the Puritans, remarked, 'If you are satisfied with an imaginary Christ you must be satisfied with an imaginary salvation.'[5]

We can be sure that we will not be allowed to slip into heaven with such faith. It will be detected and doomed.

The gracious, powerful Christ (vv. 49–50a)

THE GRACIOUSNESS OF THE LORD JESUS

Once he had discerned the deficient faith of the nobleman, we might expect to read that Jesus turned a heedless ear to his pleas. But in astonishing grace, Jesus said, 'Go your way; your son lives' (v. 50).

The Lord Jesus, who will reject false faith in the end, graciously works with us now to move us away from it. How gracious is he? Quoting from the prophet Isaiah, Matthew tells us that Jesus will not break a bruised reed or quench smoking flax (Matt. 12:20). The reed was a small musical instrument that shepherds would fashion while they were out in the field with their sheep. It worked very well until it was broken or cracked. The smoking flax was a candle that was barely flickering. Jesus has such a kind and gracious nature that he will not finish breaking a reed that is cracked or extinguish a candle that is flickering. This gracious Jesus cared enough about this nobleman to heal both his son and his faith.

The power of the Lord Jesus

It took grace for the Lord to heal this boy, but it also took power. And Jesus had the power—so much so that he healed him merely by speaking words, without even going to where the boy was.

In changing the water into wine, Jesus displayed his Lordship over time. It takes time for wine to age, but Jesus suspended the time requirement and made perfect wine on the spot.

In healing the nobleman's son, Jesus displayed his Lordship over distance. Not subject to time! Not subject to space! He is the unlimited Christ!

The Lord is still healing from a distance today. There is no greater distance than that between the holy God and sinful men and women. But in each instance of salvation, the Lord Jesus spans that greatest of all distances. From heaven's throne, he saves sinners through the work of the Holy Spirit.

The effective Christ (vv. 50b–53)

The Lord Jesus won the victory with this nobleman. He took him from little faith to great faith. The man began by believing that Jesus could work a miracle; he ended up believing that Jesus *is* the miracle—the greatest of all miracles, God in human flesh.

The work of Jesus in this man was so effective that, having heard the word of healing (v. 50), the man immediately had perfect peace. While there was still time for him to return to his home in Capernaum before dark, he evidently spent the night along the way because when he met his servants, they told him that his son was made well 'Yesterday' (v. 52)!

The work of Jesus was so effective in the heart of this man that it also led to the salvation of his family members and servants (v. 53). So this is the story of a boy being brought to the door of death so that a whole household might be brought to eternal life.

Reflect on these points

1. *We commend the nobleman for coming to Jesus and for pleading so urgently and desperately for the life of his son. But he is not the hero of this story: Jesus is.*

2. *The nobleman is an early representative of multitudes today who are not interested in God as God but rather in God as 'the fixer'.*

3. *The Lord Jesus is interested in producing true faith, and this requires him to challenge and destroy false faith.*

4. *The Lord is still healing from a distance today. From heaven's throne, he saves sinners through the work of the Holy Spirit.*

Fish and disciples caught

(Luke 5:1–11)

He said to Simon, 'Launch out into the deep and let down your nets for a catch.' But Simon answered and said to Him, 'Master, we have toiled all night and caught nothing; nevertheless at Your word I will let down the net.' And when they had done this, they caught a great number of fish, and their net was breaking.

Luke 5:4–6

This miracle was performed by Jesus at the Lake of Gennesaret, which is more commonly known as the Sea of Galilee. This lake, which was about thirteen miles long and eight miles wide, was home for Simon Peter, his brother Andrew and the sons of Zebedee (James and John).

There are two catches in this passage. One is the catch of fish, but the other is the catch of the disciples. Each of these catches drives us to think deeply about the Lord Jesus Christ.

The pursuing Christ (vv. 1–2)

Simon, Andrew, James and John had been called by the Lord to be fishers of men, but they had abandoned that new kind of fishing for their old kind. The reason may very well be that a lingering uncertainty about Jesus merged with a definite uncertainty about themselves.

If these men assumed that they could go back to their old fishing without difficulty, they were in for a shock. Fish that used to be caught with ease now refused to be caught. After a long, frustrating night of fishing without success, these men had returned to shore and begun cleaning their nets.

While they were thus occupied, Jesus turned up with a large crowd in tow. These men had abandoned the responsibility that Jesus had placed on them, but he refused to abandon them. They fled, but he pursued.

It is no small irony that the swimming fish would not be caught, but the human fish seemed to be coming after the disciples in order to be caught!

The claiming Christ (vv. 3–5)

The pursuing Jesus focused his attention on Simon Peter. He did so by laying claim to his possessions and his time. He did the former by getting into Simon's boat and teaching the people from it. He did the latter by asking Simon to get into the boat and row out from the shore. Exhausted from his night of unsuccessful fishing, Simon must have been earnestly yearning to find home and bed.

The biggest claim was still to come. After teaching for a while, Jesus staked his claim on Simon's mind by telling him to let down his nets for a catch. This was almost more than Simon could bear. Net fishing was done at night, and he and his companions had fished all night without catching a fish. Jesus was now asserting that this night activity could succeed in the daylight!

Simon knew that Jesus had been brought up in a carpenter's shop in Nazareth. What could the man possibly know about fishing? A fierce inward struggle must have ensued. Should Simon do as he was told or should he set Jesus straight? The truth is that Simon was grappling with an even greater question: was this Jesus merely a carpenter-turned-rabbi, or was he more—much more?

How many seconds did the battle rage within Simon? We do not know. We do know that he finally complied with Jesus's request. Out went the boat and down went the nets!

The Lord Jesus is still in the claiming business. He still puts his claims on the possessions and the time of his people, but his larger claim is still on our minds. He tells us to believe certain things that make no more sense to us than his command to Simon Peter to let down the nets. The Bible points to this same Jesus of Nazareth dying on a Roman cross outside Jerusalem over 2,000 years ago, and it tells us that his death on that cross is the only hope we have for the forgiveness of our sins and a right standing with God. The issue before us is whether we will accept the claim Christ puts on our thinking. Jesus claimed to know more about fishing than the fishermen, and he claims to know more about heaven and how to get into it than the intellectuals who pride themselves on their insight and scorn that cross.

The powerful Christ (vv. 6–11)

POWER OVER THE NATURAL ORDER (VV. 6–7)

Simon's nets were no sooner down than the fish who had spurned them all night began pouring in. Fish competed with one another to get in, so much so that the nets began to break. There were so many fish that Simon had to call for James and John to bring their boat out (v. 7), and even that was not enough. Both boats began to sink. No one had ever seen such a catch of fish.

There was no doubt in Simon's mind about the significance of that catch. Whatever uncertainties he had allowed himself to entertain about Jesus were now gone, wiped away by this catch as easily as cobwebs could be brushed off his hand. That catch of fish was indisputable proof that Jesus was God in human flesh and he was demonstrating his power over his creation.

The Bible promises that this Lord Jesus will finally redeem all the natural order. This world that has been so horribly affected by man's sin will at last be freed from those effects and will be restored to what it was before sin entered.

Power over the human heart (vv. 8–11)

Through this miracle, the Lord won the victory in the hearts of his disciples. Simon was particularly affected by what he had seen. It hit him with tremendous force that he was in the presence of God, and if he was in the presence of God, he was in trouble. God's presence is a holy presence and he, Simon, was anything but holy. Sinner that he was, he cried out, 'Depart from me, for I am a sinful man, O Lord!' (v. 8).

But Simon was not the only disciple affected. Luke says that all those with Simon were 'astonished' by 'the catch of fish which they had taken' (v. 9). They could no longer fish for fish. This Jesus deserved their allegiance and devotion. They must now give themselves to fishing for men (v. 10). So they 'forsook all and followed Him' (v. 11).

Reflect on these points

1. *Jesus refused to abandon his disciples. They fled, but he pursued.*

2. *Simon was grappling with this question: was this Jesus merely a carpenter-turned-rabbi, or was he more—much more?*

3. *The very Jesus who claimed to know more about fishing than the fishermen claims to know more about heaven and how to get into it than the intellectuals who pride themselves on their insight and scorn that cross.*

4. *The catch of fish was indisputable proof that Jesus was God in human flesh and he was demonstrating his power over his creation.*

Two miracles
for one man
(Mark 2:1–12)

Then they came to Him, bringing a paralytic who was carried by four men. And when they could not come near Him because of the crowd, they uncovered the roof where He was. So when they had broken through, they let down the bed on which the paralytic was lying. When Jesus saw their faith, He said to the paralytic, 'Son, your sins are forgiven you.'

Mark 2:3–5

There certainly is a lot for us to learn from the four men who carried the paralytic to Jesus. They were obviously men of compassion, faith and ingenuity. These men force us to ask ourselves some probing questions. Are we concerned about those around us? Are we seeking to bring people to the Lord? Are we willing to take unusual steps to minister?

But this passage is not primarily about these four men. It is about the Lord Jesus Christ.

The invisible miracle: spiritual healing (vv. 1–7)

The four men of this passage had heard that Jesus was in Capernaum, where he had previously preached and performed miracles. As they made their way to the house where Jesus was, they came across the paralysed man. Could not the same Jesus who had performed other miracles heal this man? With this thought in their heads, they scooped the man up and carried him along. But when they got to the house, they encountered a huge crowd, and no one would allow them to pass.

So they carried the man up to the roof, tore through it and lowered the man to Jesus (v. 4). Roofs in those days consisted of branches from trees that were covered with mud or clay that was mixed with straw, all of which would have been easy to dismantle. Access to the roof may very well have been made possible by an outside staircase or by a couple of men pulling themselves up onto the roof, where they were handed ropes by the men still on the ground. The other men would then have joined their friends on the roof to pull up the pallet of the paralysed man.

As the four men lowered the paralysed man to Jesus, they undoubtedly expected Jesus to heal the man immediately of his paralysis. They were in for a surprise. Instead, Jesus said to the paralytic, 'Son, your sins are forgiven you' (v. 5).

It is obvious that Jesus regarded this man as having a far greater problem than physical paralysis. Understanding that problem, Jesus ignored the paralysis for the moment.

Jesus understood something that we have so much difficulty discerning, namely, that this man would have been far better off remaining paralysed with his sins forgiven than to have been physically whole and not forgiven. Jesus would later state the importance of forgiveness very pointedly: 'It is better for you to enter into life lame or maimed, rather than having two hands or two feet, to be cast into the everlasting fire' (Matt. 18:8b). How we need to learn from Jesus! Eternal life is more important than anything, and eternal life can be ours only if our sins are forgiven.

The words of Jesus outraged the religious leaders who were there. They began muttering to themselves, 'Why does this

Man speak blasphemies like this? Who can forgive sins but God alone?' (v. 7).

They were right. God and God alone can forgive sins. If Jesus had not been God, they would have been correct in saying he had no right to grant forgiveness. Jesus would have been a blasphemer had he not been God! It never occurred to these men that Jesus was God in human flesh and, therefore, had the authority to forgive sins. So Jesus determined that he would give them unimpeachable evidence that he was the God-Man.

The visible miracle: physical healing (vv. 8–12)

After reading the thoughts of the religious leaders (v. 8), Jesus healed the paralysed man. He prefaced that healing by asking the religious leaders this question: 'Which is easier, to say to the paralytic, "Your sins are forgiven you," or to say, "Arise, take up your bed and walk"?' (v. 9). As he turned to the paralytic he continued, 'But that you may know that the Son of Man has power on earth to forgive sins ... I say to you, arise, take up your bed, and go to your house' (vv. 10–11). The man immediately sprang from his bed (v. 12).

So Jesus healed the man physically in order to show that he had the power and authority to heal spiritually. He healed him of his paralysis to show that he had the authority to grant forgiveness. If his word of healing had been effective, how could anyone doubt that his word of forgiveness had been as well?

There were certainly plenty of witnesses to the healing of this man. There was a large crowd there to hear Jesus, and they all saw this man who was carried to the roof on his bed later carrying that very bed as he walked out. Mark tells us that all were 'amazed' and 'glorified God, saying, "We never saw anything like this"' (v. 12).

They had not seen anything like this before because they had never seen anyone like Jesus before! God was now among men! The Eternal One had come into this temporal realm! The Creator was among his creatures! The mighty God was demonstrating his authority! The caring God was demonstrating his grace!

They marvelled at the miracle of physical healing but, as we have noted, that was the lesser miracle. The greater was the forgiveness of the man's sins. All God's people have received that miracle. Let us make sure that we are living in such a way that we demonstrate the greatness of it, that we are glorifying the God of grace who stoops to unworthy sinners and forgives them.

Reflect on these points

1. *Jesus understood that this man would have been far better off remaining paralysed with his sins forgiven than to have been physically whole and not forgiven.*

2. *Jesus was God in human flesh and, therefore, had the authority to forgive sins.*

3. *Jesus healed the man physically in order to show that he had the power and authority to heal spiritually.*

4. *All God's people have received the miracle of forgiveness of sins.*

The lame man and the God~Man

(John 5:1–15)

Now there is in Jerusalem by the Sheep Gate a pool ... Now a certain man was there who had an infirmity thirty-eight years. When Jesus saw him lying there, and knew that he already had been in that condition a long time, He said to him, 'Do you want to be made well?'

John 5:2, 5–6

The miracle of this passage is reported only in John's Gospel. It is the third of the eight related by the apostle.

The miracle itself is of a very impressive and astonishing nature. A man lame from birth is healed! But John finds in it even greater significance. This was a pivotal miracle in the attitude of the religious leaders towards Jesus. This was the miracle that so put them on the path of opposition to Jesus that there was no way back (vv. 15–18).

The lame man with a lame hope (vv. 1–5, 7)

Jesus, in Jerusalem to attend an unnamed feast, is passing by the Pool of Bethesda ('house of outpouring'). This pool, located inside the Sheep Gate of the city, was encircled by five 'porches'. These were covered colonnades.

What a sad sight greeted Jesus at the pool! It was the gathering place for the sick, the blind, the lame and the paralysed (v. 3). There were not just a few, but rather 'a great multitude'. This was a huge, depressing fellowship!

The multitude was held together by a common belief and a common hope. The belief was that an angel would come to stir the water of the pool and the first person into the pool after that stirring would be healed of his or her malady. The hope nursed by each one there was that he or she would be the first one in.

It was a strange kind of lottery: gambling on beating all the fellow-sufferers into the pool! Snatching wellness from the pool while leaving everyone else to suffer!

Mystery abounds here. The mystery of human suffering is certainly present, written in large letters. Why do we suffer at all? Why do so many suffer? Why do so many suffer so long? What causes all the pain and suffering in this world? The Bible affirms that this world is not as God originally made it. When God created it, there was no sickness or death. These things came in as a result of sin. We should not, therefore, allow the calamities of life to make us angry at God. We should rather be angry at sin. We do well to heed the words of J. C. Ryle:

> When we read of cases of sickness like this, we should remember how deeply we ought to hate sin! Sin was the original root, and cause, and fountain of every disease in the world. God did not create man to be full of aches, and pains, and infirmities. These things are the fruits of the Fall. There would have been no sickness, if there had been no sin.[1]

Then there is the mystery of this pool. Did an angel indeed stir it from time to time? If so, how did the people know when this stirring occurred? Did they actually see the angel? And was there really healing for the first person into the pool? If so, why was there healing for only the first? Why not for the first ten, fifty or hundred? Or were these people misinformed about the pool, the angel and the healing? Was it all the product of someone's fertile imagination? Were they all clinging to a false hope?

It is a fact that the oldest manuscripts of John's Gospel— and, therefore, those closest to the original manuscript—do not include the last part of verse 3 or any of verse 4. The likelihood, then, is that this whole multitude was in the grip of a superstition. How they ever came to fall into this grip we cannot say.

We know one thing for sure, though: the man to whom John calls attention was a lame man with a lame hope. Even if there was a stirring by an angel and healing for the first person into the pool, there was no hope for this man. While others were making their mad dash to the pool, the lame man could not get there (v. 7).

Yes, there is much mystery here, just as there is much mystery swirling around us today. If mystery were money, we would all be rich! But there is more than mystery here: Jesus is here, and he is here in the capacity of …

The hope of the hopeless (vv. 6, 8–15)

Jesus wades into the sea of suffering at the pool and focuses his attention on the lame man. 'Do you want to be made well?' Jesus asks (v. 6).

It appears to be a very silly question. Of course the man wanted to be made well! The man was lame. Try to find a lame person who does not desire to walk, run, leap and dance! Why would he have been at this pool if he did not desire to be well?

Let's settle it in our minds, though, that Jesus, the wisest of men, could not ask a foolish question. It was rather a very wise question. It was designed to get this man to face the harsh reality of his situation. It was intended to bring the man to the end of himself and to face his utter helplessness. It was aimed at getting this man to give up on the pool.

We all come into this world with a lameness of our own. We are spiritually lame. With this lameness, we cannot live as God made us to live. We are lamed, incapacitated, by sin, and we are completely incapable of doing anything to help ourselves. We cannot cure ourselves of spiritual lameness any more than the man at the pool could cure his physical lameness.

The spiritually lame often pin their hopes on various 'pools' such as good works or church membership for their healing. This amounts to lame people having lame hopes. The only cure for spiritual lameness is the Lord Jesus Christ. He makes the spiritually lame whole. He only does so, however, after bringing them to the end of themselves. Only those who realize their complete helplessness are saved by Christ. Only those who understand the reality and the depth of their sins are made well by him. Those who are not willing to take the place of the sinner cannot receive the Saviour. There is hope, but only for those who know their hopelessness.

After hearing the lame man's sad statement about his hopeless situation, the Lord Jesus said to him, 'Rise, take up your bed and walk' (v. 8). With splendid brevity, the apostle John writes, 'And immediately the man was made well, took up his bed, and walked' (v. 9). We should not doubt that Jesus also provided for this man an even greater healing, the healing of his soul by the forgiveness of his sins (v. 14).

So we see in Jesus once again the same grace and power that he put on display in miracle after miracle. Grace to care and power to relieve! Such grace and power do not belong to mere men. They show us that Jesus was a special man—the God-Man!

Some find it very troubling that Jesus did not heal the whole multitude of sick, blind, lame and paralysed (v. 3). He healed only one, leaving the rest to continue their dreary vigil at the pool. Others say that Jesus saw faith only in this one man. Really? It would seem that this man's faith was, like that of all the others, in the pool. The truth is that Jesus did not see faith in this man but rather created it in him.

The fact that Jesus did not heal all brings us face to face with the sovereignty of his grace. He has mercy upon whom he will have mercy (Rom. 9:15, 18). If we want to know that we are among those on whom he will have mercy, let us plead for mercy.

We might expect to read that Jesus's healing of this lame man caused joy among all the people. That was not the case. The Jews (John's shorthand for the religious leaders of Jerusalem) were incensed, believing that Jesus broke the Sabbath law by telling this man to carry his bed (v. 10). However, this was not so. Jesus had violated one of the rules that these religious leaders had attached to the Sabbath, not the law of the Sabbath itself. The Sabbath law only prohibited carrying burdens that had to do with business or gain.

The problem, then, was not with the man carrying his bed but rather with the religious leaders distorting the very law they professed to revere. These men were trusting in their faulty understanding of the law for their salvation when the real source of salvation, Jesus, was in their midst. The tragedy is that they were also lame men with a lame hope.

Reflect on these points

1. *We should not allow the calamities of life to make us angry at God.*

2. *Jesus's question was designed to bring the man to the end of himself and to face his utter helplessness. It was aimed at getting this man to give up on the pool.*

3. *We are lamed, incapacitated, by sin, and we are completely incapable of doing anything to help ourselves.*

4. *The only cure for spiritual lameness is the Lord Jesus Christ. He makes the spiritually lame whole.*

5. *The fact that Jesus did not heal all brings us face to face with the sovereignty of his grace. He has mercy upon whom he will have mercy.*

Snapshots taken on the way to the cemetery
(Luke 7:11–17)

Now it happened, the day after, that He went into a city called Nain; and many of His disciples went with Him, and a large crowd. And when He came near the gate of the city, behold, a dead man was being carried out, the only son of his mother; and she was a widow.

Luke 7:11–12

This passage records for us the first of three instances in which Jesus raised someone from the dead. The others are the daughter of Jairus (Matt. 9:18–26; Mark 5:21–43; Luke 8:40–56) and Lazarus (John 11:1–44). It also relates the first resurrection in a very long time, the last having occurred around nine hundred years earlier during the ministry of Elisha (2 Kings 4:18–37).

In addition to meeting the need of the moment, this miracle provides marvellous pictures—or snapshots—of the things that the Lord Jesus will eventually do for all his people.

Tears removed (vv. 11–13)

Here is a very sad situation. A widow has lost her only son. The joy of her life is now gone, along with her financial security. Death, the cruellest of tyrants, makes no distinctions and softens none of its blows. It makes no exceptions and grants no waivers. It has no regard for the most tender of human ties. It snatches the son of this woman, leaves her life in ruin, and smiles while doing so.

Why do we have death? Some blame God, but the real fault

lies with sin. If there had been no sin, there would have been no death. It is as simple as that.

Jesus, accompanied by a large crowd (v. 11), was approaching the gate of the city. The widow, also accompanied by a large crowd (v. 13), was going from the city to the cemetery. Touched by this scene of misery, Jesus said to the woman, 'Do not weep' (v. 13).

'Don't cry' is a common plea that we often use with family members and friends. But while we tell loved ones not to cry, we often have no way to remove the reason for their tears. It was different with Jesus. His words to the widow carried with them the promise that he was about to remedy the situation.

No one had asked Jesus to do anything. There is no suggestion that anyone among the mourners knew him. He could have chosen merely to stand to one side as those mourners passed by, or been content to offer a word of condolence. But his sympathetic heart compelled him to do more—much more! The Bible assures us that Jesus's heart has not changed since that day (Heb. 4:15).

The picture or prophecy at this point is of that coming day when the Lord will wipe away all the tears of his people (Rev. 21:4).

Death conquered (vv. 14–15)

After telling the widow not to weep, Jesus stepped up to the open coffin of her son, touched him and said, 'Young man, I say to you, arise' (v. 14). That was all it took! Luke says, 'So he who was dead sat up and began to speak' (v. 15).

This element of the story provides us with a picture of what is to come for the children of God. The same Jesus who raised this young man will come again 'with a shout', and 'the dead in Christ will rise' (1 Thes. 4:16).

What will Jesus shout? It may very well be one word: 'Arise!'

There will, however, be a monumental difference on that day. The widow's son was raised to resume life as he had known it before he died, and he would, therefore, have to die again. But when Jesus returns, his people will be raised to enter a whole new kind of life, and they will never have to die again.

Ties restored (v. 15)

After raising the young man from the dead, Jesus 'presented him to his mother' (v. 15).

This part of the story calls us to look again towards the second coming of Jesus. The apostle Paul tells us that after dead believers are raised from their graves, living believers will be 'caught up together with them in the clouds to meet the Lord in the air' (1 Thes. 4:17). The great joy of that day will be meeting the Lord, but next to it will be the joy of getting our Christian loved ones back. S. G. DeGraaf writes of that time, 'Then we shall see that our ties on earth were not just temporal and meaningless but we shall discover their sanctified, glorified meaning.'[1] Alexander Maclaren observes of Jesus, 'If He raised this boy from the dead that his mother's arms might twine round him again, and his mother's heart be comforted, will He not in that great Resurrection give back dear ones to empty, outstretched arms, and thereby quiet hungry hearts?'[2]

God glorified (vv. 16–17)

Luke closes his account of this miracle by describing the response of the people who witnessed it, and we must note again that it was performed in the presence of many, many witnesses. What was the nature of their response? Luke tells us that they 'glorified God' (v. 16).

That response provides us with our final picture of the saints glorifying their Lord in heaven, and that response, boisterous and joyful as it was, will be faint when compared with the praises God's people will offer then (Rev. 5:12–14; 15:3–4).

We have seen in the raising of the widow's son glimpses of our own future if we belong to the Lord. The future of those who do not know Christ will be radically different. Tears will never be dried. Death will be endless. Human ties will never be restored. But God will still be glorified. The bottom line is that each of us will bring glory either to God's grace or to his justice.

Reflect on these points

1. *Death has no regard for the most tender of human ties.*

2. *While we tell loved ones not to cry, we often have no way to remove the reason for their tears. It was different with Jesus.*

3. *The same Jesus who raised this young man will come again 'with a shout', and 'the dead in Christ will rise' (1 Thes. 4:16).*

4. *When Jesus comes, our greatest joy will be meeting him, but next to it will be the joy of getting our Christian loved ones back.*

5. *Each of us will bring glory either to God's grace or to his justice.*

The wonder of Jesus
(Mark 4:35–41)

On the same day, when evening had come, He said to them, 'Let us cross over to the other side.' Now when they had left the multitude, they took Him along in the boat as He was ... And a great windstorm arose, and the waves beat into the boat, so that it was already filling. But He was in the stern, asleep on a pillow. And they awoke Him and said to Him, 'Teacher, do You not care that we are perishing?'

Mark 4:35–38

It may very well be that Jesus's disciples had been with him long enough that a dull familiarity had set in and their awe of him had begun to fade. In the episode described in these verses, the disciples got their awe back.

This experience took them from fear to fear. They began by fearing the storm, and they ended up fearing Jesus. That is evident in their cry, 'Who can this be, that even the wind and the sea obey Him!' (v. 41). This is an exclamation of astonishment, of wondering awe. They were confronted with, and amazed by, the wonder of Jesus.

Because believers in Christ can so easily settle into a state of dull familiarity with the Lord Jesus, we too urgently need to get the wonder of him back, just as much as did those disciples of old.

The wonder of God in human flesh
Mark, the author of this Gospel, leaves no doubt about the wonder that he wanted his readers to have regarding Jesus: it was the wonder of God in human flesh. Jesus was the God-

Man. Fully God! Fully man (1:1, 11; 3:11; 5:7; 9:7; 14:61–62; 15:39)!

We have all the evidence we need for this in the miracle before us. Men do not by mere words hush violent winds and calm turbulent seas—but Jesus did! Three little words—'Peace, be still!'—stopped the wind in its tracks and so levelled the waves that they were like a pane of glass.

This same powerful Christ calls us to obey his Word. Is it a wise thing to refuse the Word that the wind and waves obey? There is something far greater for us to fear than the various storms or crises of life and that is the Lord who rules the storms. Even the wind and waves have enough sense to obey his Word. Do we have that much sense?

The wonder of God in the storm

To say that Jesus was God in human flesh is to say that he came into the human arena to experience all that is common to humanity, and nothing is more common to humanity than storms.

Some would have us believe that being Jesus's disciples means that we should not have any difficulties in life. This passage says otherwise. These men, disciples of Jesus, were in the process of following his command (v. 35) and they were in trouble! Charles Erdman is correct in saying, 'To follow the Master does not mean "smooth sailing" always, or cloudless skies.'[1]

What a consolation it must have been to the disciples to see Jesus there in the boat with them! But their sense of consolation began to fade and their anxiety began to rise. This was a fierce storm, and Jesus was sleeping as if it were perfectly quiet. When they reached their breaking point, they cried out, 'Teacher, do You not care that we are perishing?' (v. 38).

Then they discovered the wonder of God in the storm. This Jesus, who was God in flesh, did care! The humanity of Jesus means not only that he can sympathize with us in our trials, but also that he cannot help but sympathize with us (Heb. 4:15).

How can we be sure that God cares for us in the storms of life? The answer is found in the death of his Son on the cross. Through that death, the Lord Jesus has already stilled the greatest of all our storms—the storm of the eternal wrath of God (Rom. 5:9; 1 Thes. 1:10). Why should we doubt for a single moment that he is willing to still our lesser storms?

After the storm was stilled, Jesus rebuked his disciples for their fearfulness and lack of faith (v. 40). This is also a proof of his care. By rebuking their little faith, he was moving them towards greater faith, and in doing so was preparing them to receive even greater blessings.

The wonder of God in eternal glory

This passage begins with Jesus saying to his disciples, 'Let us cross over to the other side' (v. 35). That word carried with it the assurance that they would make it through the storm. Although they had their moments of doubt during the storm, they did indeed make it safely to the other side.

A day is coming when the Lord Jesus will say to each of his people, 'Let us cross over to the other side.' Part of the glory of that day will be the peace of knowing that our storms are for ever over.

Another part of the glory of that day will be finding that this natural realm has itself been renewed and restored. Why do we have storms in this life? It is because the first Adam fell into sin and caused all creation to be marred by sin. Jesus is the Second Adam (and the last!). He will reverse for his people what the first Adam did, which means, among other things, that he will restore all nature to what it was before sin entered this world (Rom. 8:19–22).

Nature was rising up against his disciples to threaten them, but Jesus rose up and calmed it. In showing his authority over the wind and the waves, Jesus was giving his disciples a preview of that day when he will finally still all of nature for the last time and his people will dwell in perfect security on a new earth.

While we will most certainly rejoice in heaven in the glory of being storm-free and of this natural realm being made new, our greatest rejoicing will come from being in the presence of the Lord Jesus, who will have accomplished all these things for us. The greatest glory of Glory will be the Lord of Glory.

Reflect on these points

1. *There is something far greater for us to fear than the various storms or crises of life and that is the Lord who rules the storms.*

2. *The humanity of Jesus means not only that he can sympathize with us in our trials, but also that he cannot help but sympathize with us (Heb. 4:15).*

3. *A day is coming when the Lord Jesus will say to each of his people, 'Let us cross over to the other side.'*

4. *The greatest glory of Glory will be the Lord of Glory.*

Victory over
the devil
(Mark 5:1–20)

Then they came to the other side of the sea, to the country of the Gadarenes. And when He had come out of the boat, immediately there met Him out of the tombs a man with an unclean spirit, who had his dwelling among the tombs; and no one could bind him, not even with chains ... ; neither could anyone tame him. And always, night and day, he was in the mountains and in the tombs, crying out and cutting himself with stones.

Mark 5:1–5

The miracle recorded in these verses was performed by Jesus in 'the country of the Gadarenes', which was located on 'the other side of the sea' (v. 1), that is, the Sea of Galilee. This was a Gentile area, and the devil was especially strong there.

Many doubt that there is such a being as Satan. Meanwhile, we see evidence of his reality all around us. At a later point in his ministry, the Lord Jesus would refer to the devil as 'a strong man' and to himself as One 'stronger than he' (Luke 11:21–22).

In this passage, we see both the strength of the devil and the far greater strength of the Lord Jesus.

Jesus and the demon-possessed man (vv. 1–12)

When Jesus and his disciples arrived in Gadara, they were immediately met with a most pitiful and gruesome sight. A man possessed with 'an unclean spirit' (v. 2) came out of the tombs. This was an area of cliffs in which were caves that were used for tombs. This man made his home in those caves.

The man posed a real threat to the people in the community. They tried to bind him but, possessing superhuman strength, he easily snapped their chains and shackles (vv. 3–4). This indicates something of the great power of Satan. We are also told that this poor man was constantly crying out in extreme anguish and was cutting himself with stones (v. 5). This indicates something of the cruelty of Satan.

It is interesting that the demoniac recognized Jesus from afar and 'ran and worshiped Him' (v. 6). While Satan is a powerful foe, he knows that he is not more powerful than God, and Jesus was and is God. The devil also knows that he is destined to experience eternal torment. Here he expressed the fear that Jesus had come to implement that torment (v. 7). The fact that Satan knew the truth about Jesus and about eternal torment means that he is a better theologian than the seminary professors and pastors who question these things.

We get to the root of the situation when this man responded to Jesus's asking his name by saying, 'My name is Legion; for we are many' (v. 9). A Roman legion consisted of 6,000 soldiers!

Knowing that Jesus was going to drive them out of the man, the demons began to beg him not to send them 'out of the country' but into a nearby herd of pigs (vv. 10–12).

Jesus and the pigs (v. 13)

Why did the demons desire to go into the pigs? They may

very well have feared, as noted above, that Jesus had come to cast them into hell. Some believe that it was because they are disembodied spirits and, as such, desire to possess some kind of body. Knowing that Jesus would not let them possess another human being, the demons decided that the pigs were the next best option!

It is also possible that Satan was here resorting to Plan B. He is never without plans! If Jesus allowed his demons to go into the pigs, Satan felt sure that the Gadarenes would turn against Jesus and he, Satan, would be able to keep his grip on that area.

Jesus's consent to the demons' request has confounded and mystified many. Why did he sanction the destruction of 2,000 animals when he could have driven the demons away without it? Some who have bacon or sausage for breakfast and pork chops for supper wring their hands over this event and eagerly conclude that Jesus cares nothing for animals!

So what can we say about Jesus's reasons for complying with the demons' plea? One answer is that in doing so, Jesus gave a powerful and vivid picture of Satan's power to destroy and of his own power to deliver. How people today, especially young people, need to learn that Satan is a destroyer! He does not bring happiness; he ruins it. And how people need to learn that Jesus alone can deliver us from the tyranny of Satan!

Another answer is that Jesus was setting the stage for the Gadarenes to make a choice. Would those people prize their pigs or would they prize Jesus?

Jesus and the citizens (vv. 14–20)

With the demon-possessed man now sitting before them in perfect peace and tranquillity, and with their pigs in the sea, the Gadarenes made their choice. The loss of their pigs touched them far more deeply than the deliverance of the man who had posed such a threat to their community. They would rather have their pigs and terror than have Jesus and peace. So they 'began to plead with Him to depart from their region' (v. 17).

Many repeat the error of the Gadarenes. They would much rather have sin and all the hurt it produces than have Christ.

Jesus did depart but, in an act of kindness that those citizens did not deserve, he left as his witness the man whom he had delivered (vv. 18–20).

The drama reported in Mark's account of this miracle is still being played out. Satan is still destroying, Jesus is still delivering and many people are still preferring Satan over Jesus. This drama will continue until the end. At that time, the same Jesus who won the victory over Satan at Gadara will finally and completely banish him (Rev. 20:10), and those who spent their lives preferring Satan will share his doom (Matt. 25:41).

Reflect on these points

1. *While Satan is a powerful foe, he himself knows that he is not more powerful than God, and Jesus was and is God.*

2. *By allowing the demons to enter the pigs, Jesus gave a powerful and vivid picture of Satan's power to destroy and of his own power to deliver.*

3. *Like the Gadarenes, many would much rather have sin and all the hurt it produces than have Christ.*

4. *The Lord Jesus will be victorious over Satan at the end of time, and those who chose Satan in this life will share his judgement.*

A miracle that ended twelve long years
(Mark 5:25–34)

Now a certain woman had a flow of blood for twelve years, and had suffered many things from many physicians. She had spent all that she had and was no better, but rather grew worse. When she heard about Jesus, she came behind Him in the crowd and touched His garment. For she said, 'If only I may touch His clothes, I shall be made well.'

Mark 5:25–28

The second half of the fifth chapter of Mark's Gospel introduces us to two people whose previous twelve years were totally different. We first meet Jairus, who was 'one of the rulers of the synagogue' (v. 22). The previous twelve years of this man's life were brightened by his little girl. How much joy she had brought him! How he loved her! But now she was ill, so critically ill that she was near death (v. 23). Jairus found Jesus and 'begged Him earnestly' to come and heal his daughter.

Next we meet 'a certain woman' (v. 25). While Jesus was on his way to Jairus's house, he was interrupted and detained by this woman who had had 'a flow of blood for twelve years' (v. 25).

Do twelve years constitute a long period or a short one? It depends. If you are sick during those years, as was the woman in this passage, they are very long. If, as was the case with Jairus, you lose a twelve-year-old child to death, those years are very short indeed.

Each situation—the twelve long years and the twelve short ones—represented crushing human need. The good news is that the Lord Jesus was sufficient for each need.

From hopelessness to hope (vv. 25–28)

Mark wants us to understand how pathetic and hopeless this woman's situation was. Hers was double suffering. During the twelve years she had suffered from her illness, she had also suffered 'many things from many physicians' (v. 26). Mark drives home her hopelessness with these stark words: 'She had spent all that she had and was no better, but rather grew worse.'

One day, a ray of hope broke though the dark clouds of her hopelessness. This was the day that 'she heard about Jesus' (v. 27). What did she hear about him? It is safe to say that she heard about the power of Jesus to handle hopeless situations. As she listened, a plan was born. She would go and touch him and be made well.

The fact that Jesus was accompanied by a large crowd worked to her advantage. She did not want to be detected. Her disease caused her, as well as anyone who touched her, to be ceremonially unclean.

From illness to wellness (v. 29)

The woman succeeded in her plan. She worked her way through the multitude and touched Jesus. One touch was all that it took: she immediately knew that she had been healed.

Here again we are called to marvel at the power, knowledge and grace of Jesus. His power is evident in the instantaneous and complete healing of the woman. We should note, however, that this healing power resided in Jesus and not in his garment.

His knowledge is evident in that he recognized the touch of this woman amid all the 'touches' that he was receiving (v. 31).

His grace is evident in that he was willing to grant healing to this woman, even though she obviously came with a flawed faith that viewed him as some sort of magician instead of the Son of God.

From hiding to telling (vv. 30–34)

After Jesus felt the touch of this woman, he turned and asked the crowd, 'Who touched My clothes? (v. 30).

We must always remember that, when the Lord Jesus asks a question, it is not because he does not know the answer. His purpose in asking was to bring the woman from anonymity to testimony. She wanted to clutch her blessing and steal away, but the Lord Jesus wanted her to bear witness to her blessing and, in doing so, bring glory to God and help to others.

'Fearing and trembling', the woman came forward, fell at his feet and 'told Him the whole truth' (v. 33). She must have feared that Jesus would scold her, but he only added to her blessing (v. 34).

We must see these various details of Jesus's ministry in the larger context of his purpose for coming to this earth (Matt. 1:21; Luke 19:10). With Jesus's saving purpose in mind, we can see certain parallels between his healing of this woman and his saving of sinners.

Let's take this woman as an emblem of every sinner. Her condition was horrible and there was no one to help her. The sinner's condition is even more horrible. He or she is already condemned and under the wrath of God (John 3:18, 36). Like the woman, the sinner may very well go from doctor to doctor (Dr Good Works, Dr Church Membership, Dr Feel-Good Religion), only to find no help.

Let's take what this woman did as an emblem of what every sinner must do. She came to Jesus with an imperfect faith. To be saved, the sinner must come to Jesus. He or she does not have to have perfect theology. The sinner only needs to know that he or she is a great sinner and that Jesus is a great Saviour.

Let's take what Jesus did for this woman as an emblem of what he will do for every sinner who comes to him. Just as he completely delivered this woman from her physical problem, so he will completely deliver the sinner from spiritual death and from the sentence of eternal wrath (Rom. 5:9; 8:1).

Let's take Jesus's willingness to share the woman's uncleanness as a picture of his death on the cross. There he shared our uncleanness so he could deliver us from it. On that cross, he received the wrath of God so that all who believe in him will not have to endure that wrath themselves.

Let's take Jesus's requiring this woman to confess as a picture of the confession that he demands from all who receive him as their Lord and Saviour (Matt. 10:32–33; 2 Tim. 2:12).

Reflect on these points

1. *This woman had endured double suffering. She had suffered from her illness for twelve years, and throughout these years she had suffered 'many things from many physicians'.*

2. *This miracle calls us to marvel again at the power, knowledge and grace of Jesus.*

3. *To be saved, the sinner must come to Jesus. He or she does not have to have perfect theology. The sinner only needs to know that he or she is a great sinner and that Jesus is a great Saviour.*

4. *On the cross, Jesus shared our uncleanness so that he could deliver us from it.*

A miracle that prolonged twelve short years
(Mark 5:21–24, 35–43)

Now when Jesus had crossed over again by boat to the other side, a great multitude gathered to Him; and He was by the sea. And behold, one of the rulers of the synagogue came, Jairus by name. And when he saw Him, he fell at His feet and begged Him earnestly, saying, 'My little daughter lies at the point of death. Come and lay Your hands on her, that she may be healed, and she will live.'

Mark 5:21–23

As Jesus finished dealing with the woman who had touched his garment, messengers came to Jairus and bluntly said, 'Your daughter is dead' (v. 35). This girl was twelve years of age (v. 42). She was born at the same time the woman with the haemorrhage had begun to suffer. As we saw in the last chapter, to the woman, those were twelve very long years, but when Jairus received the jarring news of his daughter's death, those same twelve years must have seemed a very brief time indeed.

Mark's account centres on three statements that Jesus made in connection with the girl's death.

The statement that produced hope: 'Do not be afraid; only believe' (v. 36)

The messengers took it upon themselves to do more than announce the girl's death; they also pronounced the situation to be hopeless, asking Jairus, 'Why trouble the Teacher any further?' (v. 35). To them, death was final and irreversible.

They would have said, 'Where there's life, there's hope.' But there was now no life, so there was no hope!

The messengers said that there was no need to 'trouble' Jesus, but death is no trouble for him. Before Jairus could slide into the mire of despair, Jesus said, 'Do not be afraid; only believe' (v. 36).

Precious words! Jairus had already shown faith in Jesus by seeking him out. Now his faith was beginning to crumble and he sorely needed Jesus's reassuring words. Jesus was simply saying, 'You have believed up to this point, so don't stop now. Keep believing.'

What the gloomy messengers did not understand—and what Jairus was about to misunderstand—was that there is no need to place limits on the power of the Lord Jesus. He is just as able to raise the dead as he is to heal the sick.

The statement that produced scorn: 'The child is not dead, but sleeping' (v. 39)

When Jesus arrived at Jairus's house, he found that the professional mourners had already gathered and were engaging in their customary shrieking and wailing. We should not be surprised that they were so quickly on the scene. In those days, the dead had to be buried without delay. There was no time to lose.

Jesus astounded these mourners when he told them that the little girl was only sleeping. These people were around death all the time; they knew it when they saw it. So they laughed at Jesus.

But this was a special occasion. Sleep is something from which people awaken, and Jesus was about to awaken this girl. The mourners thought that they knew better than Jesus, but he knew better than they.

How many today are like these mourners, thinking that they know better than the Lord on such things as sin, judgement, salvation and eternity. They will eventually learn what the mourners learned: Jesus knows better than mere mortals.

Death was also a sleep for Jesus himself: he sprang from the grave on the third day to enjoy glorious resurrection life. Death is also a sleep for all his people: they will share his resurrection life when he comes again (1 Thes. 4:13–18).

Jesus was unfazed by the ridicule of these mourners. He simply 'put them all outside' (v. 40). The Lord is also unfazed by all the ridicule that people today are heaping upon his teachings. He merely laughs at the scoffing of the godless (Ps. 2:4) and he will eventually put them outside—out into eternal destruction (2 Thes. 1:8–10).

The statement that produced victory: 'Little girl, I say to you, arise' (v. 41)

With the mourners out of the way, Jesus went into the room where the girl was lying, took her by the hand and spoke the above words. The young girl immediately awoke, got up and started walking.

Note that, by touching her, Jesus made himself ceremonially unclean. He shared her uncleanness so that he could deliver her from it. This is a picture of what he would do on the cross for sinners.

Now we know the truth about Jesus. He has authority over death, and he has that authority because he is God. He demonstrated that same authority again when he arose from his grave. Paul declares that Jesus's resurrection proved that he was the Son of God 'with power' (Rom. 1:4). With this power to conquer death, Jesus has promised to raise to everlasting life all those who trust him as their Lord and Saviour (John 14:19; 1 Cor. 15:20–28). By raising this girl, Jesus was giving notice to Satan and all his hosts that he will eventually raid death of all those who believe in him.

The witnesses of this miracle (v. 40) were 'overcome with great amazement' (v. 42). That will surely be the response of all God's people when they rise from their graves to meet the Lord in the air.

Jesus commanded those who saw the miracle to keep it quiet. Of course, the people in the community would know about the miracle just by seeing the girl walking around. Jesus's command, then, should be taken to mean that he did not want the news to go beyond that community. Premature Messiah talk would cause the people to declare him to be their earthly king. Jesus had a different task and a different timetable.

Reflect on these points

1. *Death is no trouble for Jesus.*

2. *There is never any need to place limits on the power of Jesus. He is just as able to raise the dead as he is to heal the sick.*

3. *The Lord is unfazed by all the ridicule that people today are heaping upon his teachings. He merely laughs at the scoffing of the godless (Ps. 2:4) and he will eventually put them outside—out into eternal destruction (2 Thes. 1:8–10).*

4. *By raising this girl, Jesus was giving notice to Satan and all his hosts that he will eventually raid death of all those who believe in him.*

A miracle of multiplication
(John 6:1–15)

... Jesus lifted up His eyes, and seeing a great multitude coming toward Him, He said to Philip, 'Where shall we buy bread, that these may eat?' ... Philip answered Him, 'Two hundred denarii worth of bread is not sufficient for them, that every one of them may have a little.' One of His disciples, Andrew, Simon Peter's brother, said to Him, 'There is a lad here who has five barley loaves and two small fish, but what are they among so many?'

John 6:5, 7–9

J esus did many, many miracles, but this one alone is reported in all four Gospels. The Holy Spirit, who is the ultimate Author of Scripture, evidently wanted to emphasize the special nature of this miracle. What made it so very special?

It put special focus on Jesus's compassion (vv. 1–5)

The Gospel accounts make it plain that Jesus had gone into the wilderness so that he and his disciples could rest (Matt. 14:13; Mark 6:30–31; Luke 9:10). The multitude had a different idea. They followed Jesus into this desolate place 'because they saw His signs which He performed on those who were diseased' (John 6:2). Some undoubtedly came because they needed healing, while others just wanted to see healings.

Jesus could easily have been exasperated with these people, most of whom craved the sensational and all of whom had interrupted his time of solitude. But Jesus was never able to look on a multitude with an uncaring heart (Matt. 9:36; Mark 6:34). So he began to teach and heal (Mark 6:34; Luke 9:11).

How Jesus tests his people on this matter of compassion! Matthew tells us that Jesus also seized such opportunities to drive home to his disciples the greatness of the spiritual harvest and the need for labourers (Matt. 9:37–38).

The same compassion that drove Jesus to teach and heal also caused him to take note of the situation. It was now late, the people were hungry and the place was so remote that food was not attainable. Jesus could not ignore such need.

It put special focus on Jesus's wisdom (vv. 5–9)

Jesus knew that there was more to be done than simply feeding the multitude: his disciples also needed to be further trained. So Jesus put this question to Philip: 'Where shall we buy bread, that these may eat?' (v. 5).

The Lord often presents his people with problems and trials so they can see if they have truly learned to rely on him or if they are still depending on themselves. Philip should have known that when Jesus asked a question, it was not because he did not know the answer. Philip should have recognized the test and answered by saying something of this nature: 'Lord, I have seen you do all kinds of miracles up to this day and even on this day. I know that you are more than sufficient to meet the need of this moment.'

However, Philip failed to recognize the test and therefore failed it. After running a quick calculation, he announced that two hundred denarii would be required just to give each person 'a little' (v. 7). How foolish to speak of 'a little' in the presence of the One who had so frequently demonstrated his power to abundantly bless!

As Philip announced his feeble calculation, Andrew brought to Jesus a lad with five barley loaves and two small fish (vv. 8–9). Andrew's question—'… what are they among so many?'—shows that he was thinking in terms of division when he should have been thinking in terms of multiplication. He also had seen Jesus do many mighty things.

It put special focus on Jesus's power (vv. 10–15)

Putting aside the failings of his disciples, Jesus commanded them to have the multitude seated. He took the boy's loaves and fish, gave thanks and handed them to the disciples. As the disciples distributed food to the people, the food multiplied to the point that all ate 'as much as they wanted' (v. 11).

Some see the lad as the hero of this story. As far as they are concerned, the big point here is that this boy was willing to give his lunch to Jesus; therefore, we too should always be willing to give whatever we have to Jesus. However, our focus should not be on the lad but on the Lord. Who is this One who could feed a multitude from so little? It is Jesus, God in human flesh! What power is this that could do so much from so little? It is the power of the Lord of Glory!

It put special focus on the true work of Jesus's disciples

This miracle shows us that Jesus's followers, especially those who are ministers of the gospel, should understand that they are in the distribution business. The Jesus who provided physical bread on this occasion is himself the spiritual Bread that sinners need to give them spiritual life. The job of ministers of the gospel is to be ministers of the gospel. It is their job—and glorious privilege—to distribute far and wide the saving message of Jesus Christ. They are not to come up with their own message and distribute that; they are to distribute what they receive from the Lord Jesus himself, namely, the truth that he is the Bread of life.

When Jesus was testing his disciples on the matter of feeding the multitude, the disciples, according to Mark, advised Jesus to send the multitude away (Mark 6:36). But Jesus responded, 'You give them something to eat' (v. 37). Many preachers these days are sending the spiritually hungry multitudes away to entertainment, psychology and principles for coping with life. Yet there is never any need to send people away from Jesus: he is everything they need. So the need is to give people what they need: Jesus.

We take our leave of the feeding of the five thousand by thinking about another event that put the compassion, wisdom and power of God on display to an even larger degree: Jesus's death on the cross. Was God's compassion there? It certainly was. Jesus went to the cross because of the pity God feels towards helpless sinners. Was the wisdom of God there? Yes, it was. The cross of Christ wisely resolved the most profound of all dilemmas, namely, satisfying the demands of both God's justice and his grace. The demands of justice were satisfied because God poured out his wrath on Jesus in the stead of his people, and his grace was satisfied because the fact that Jesus received God's wrath in the place of sinners means that there is no wrath left for those sinners. Was the power of God there? It was. By means of Jesus dying on the cross, God actually provided the way of saving sinners.

The cross of Jesus is the message that is given to the church to distribute to this world, and it is her immense privilege to do so.

Reflect on these points

1. *Jesus was never able to look on a multitude with an uncaring heart.*

2. *The Lord often presents his people with problems and trials so they can see if they have truly learned to rely on him or if they are still depending on themselves.*

3. *The job of ministers of the gospel is to be ministers of the gospel. It is their job—and glorious privilege—to distribute far and wide the saving message of Jesus Christ.*

4. *There is never any need to send people away from Jesus: he is everything they need. So the need is to give people what they need: Jesus.*

A string of wonders
(Matt. 14:22–33;
Mark 6:45–52;
John 6:15–21)

Now when evening came, His disciples went down to the sea, got into the boat, and went over the sea toward Capernaum. And it was already dark, and Jesus had not come to them. Then the sea arose because a great wind was blowing. So when they had rowed about three or four miles, they saw Jesus walking on the sea and drawing near the boat; and they were afraid.

John 6:16–19

J esus's feeding of the multitude caused the smouldering embers of messianic hope to break into full flame. The people were ready to declare Jesus their king on the spot (John 6:15).

Jesus as king! What could be wrong with that? Everything was wrong! It would have made Jesus the wrong kind of king in the wrong kind of kingdom. They were thinking in terms of Jesus as the head of a political, material kingdom. He would throw off Roman oppression, make Israel supreme among the nations and feed his subjects every day. That was what they wanted from their Messiah.

Jesus would have none of this. He was a king all right—King of kings and Lord of lords! But he never came to this earth to set up and rule over a temporal kingdom. His kingdom is not of this world (John 18:36).

So Jesus took charge of the situation. He 'made' his disciples get into a boat and start rowing towards Capernaum on the other side of the lake, and he 'sent the multitudes away' (Matt. 14:22).

How does one disperse a multitude that is at a fever pitch

of excitement? It was no problem for Jesus. His authoritative word was enough! Was there a miracle in that authoritative dispersing? Perhaps so!

Then Jesus 'went up on a mountain by Himself to pray' (Matt. 14:23). While Jesus was praying, his disciples were rowing. How they rowed! They were rowing for their lives because they were in the midst of a 'contrary' wind (Matt. 14:24). Crossing the lake should have taken only an hour or two, but several hours had passed and the disciples were still at it!

The stage was now set for a cluster of miracles or a string of wonders, the first of which was …

Jesus walking on water

Jesus was aware of the disciples' struggle in the storm. Mark tells us that he saw them 'straining at rowing' while he was still 'on the land' (Mark 6:47–48). Why did Jesus let the storm rage all about them? Why did he let them struggle so? Do we not have to say that he was teaching them something through that storm? Was he not drilling it into their minds and hearts that the crowd had it all wrong? That he had not come to set up a kingdom of comfort that would free his subjects from difficulties? Following him would not mean ease but hardship.

Of this we can be sure: the Lord Jesus still uses difficulties to teach and discipline his people. He always does so out of a heart of love for them and with their best interests in mind.

In his own time, Jesus came to his disciples. How he came! Walking through the storm on the rolling, churning waves!

How did the disciples respond to this sight? They were terrified! They thought they were seeing a ghost (Matt. 14:26; Mark 6:49)! They had seen Jesus feed a multitude only a few hours earlier, but they did not believe that a multitude-feeder could be a water-walker. Mark says that their 'heart was hardened' (Mark 6:52).

God had used Moses to make a path through the Red Sea and to feed the Israelites with manna in the wilderness. If, in the feeding of the five thousand, the disciples had seen Jesus as greater than Moses, they should not have been surprised to see him, in Moses-like fashion, making a path through the sea.

The second of the wonders on this occasion was …

Jesus enabling Simon Peter to walk on the water

All the disciples were scared out of their wits at the sight of Jesus. That included Simon. But Jesus spoke these words of assurance: 'Be of good cheer! It is I; do not be afraid' (Matt. 14:27; Mark 6:50).

Those words were enough for Simon to collect himself and say, 'Lord, if it is You, command me to come to You on the water' (Matt. 14:28). Jesus responded with one word: 'Come' (v. 29). And Simon began to walk on the water! It was not a matter of Simon doing this on his own, but rather of Jesus enabling him to do it. Those very disciples would themselves conduct ministries that would be marked by the miraculous (2 Cor. 12:12; Heb. 2:4), but the power to do such things would not come from them but from their Lord. While believers today are not miracle-working apostles, we can rest assured that our Lord still supplies us with enabling grace so we can live for him.

Simon Peter did well until he took his eyes off the Lord and began to take note of the wind and the waves. Then he began to sink. Even a good swimmer like Simon would have been no match for this stormy water, but there was no need for Simon to fear. The Lord who had enabled him also rescued him (Matt. 14:30–31).

What a Christ we have! By enabling Simon Peter to walk on the water, Jesus was providing his disciples of every age with a picture of the final age in which he will free all nature from the ravages of sin and will share his conquest with all his people. While Simon's mastery of the water lasted just a moment, the saints' eventual mastery of all creation will last for ever.

Jesus stilling the storm

After Jesus rescued Simon Peter from drowning, the two of them got into the boat and, in the words of Matthew's Gospel, 'the wind ceased' (Matt. 14:32).

We should not doubt that this was yet another miracle. The storm that had been raging so violently for so many hours stopped and all was calm. Just as Jesus calmed a storm on an earlier occasion (Matt. 8:23–27; Mark 4:35–41; Luke 8:22–25), so he did again here. On the previous occasion, Jesus was in the boat with his disciples when the storm arose, but on this occasion, as we have noted, he came to them in the storm.

The lesson is the same in both situations: Jesus is Lord over all creation. This fact, so amply demonstrated again in his mastery of this particular storm, gave the disciples much to think about. Yes, they had in the stilling of this storm yet another proof that Jesus was God, and Matthew tells us that they 'worshiped Him, saying, "Truly, You are the Son of God"' (Matt. 14:33).

But Jesus had stilled this storm only a few hours after he fed the five thousand and in doing so kindled messianic fervour in the hearts of the multitude and of his disciples. Therefore, his quieting of the storm must have caused the disciples to ponder deeply this question: why would the King of all creation be willing to settle for being king over a mere earthly realm? They must have reasoned along these lines: if Jesus is Lord over a storm, he is Lord over all the natural order, and if he is Lord over the natural order, he does not have to settle for being Lord over a political kingdom. So Jesus hushed not only the storm but also, for the moment, the disciples' interest in him setting up a temporal kingdom.

Jesus landing the boat

The Gospel of John adds yet another detail to this 'string of wonders', namely, that the boat was immediately 'at the land where they were going' (John 6:21). So Jesus did in an instant what the disciples had been unable to do in hours and hours of rowing! William Hendriksen writes of Jesus, ' ... he conquers even space, for when he enters the boat, it is on the shore *all at once*'[1] (italics are his).

This landing put the disciples at rest. Now their rowing was over. Now their anxiety about whether the storm would finish their lives was ended. Now their questions about whether Jesus was truly the King were all answered. They were safely at rest on the shore.

We have no trouble relating the last of this string of miracles to ourselves. Life in this world is such that we Christians often feel as if we are in a terrific storm and, not realizing as we should the Lord's purposes in allowing our difficulties, we easily conclude that he does not care for us. But the Lord knows about our storms, and he cares for us in the midst of the storms. In his own time, he will come to help us. J. C. Ryle writes,

> Let all true Christians take comfort in the thought that their Saviour is Lord of waves and winds, of storms and tempests, and can come to them in the darkest hour, 'walking upon the sea'. There are waves of trouble far heavier than any on the Lake of Galilee. There are days of darkness which try the faith of the holiest Christian. But let us never despair if Christ is our Friend. He can come to our aid in an hour when we think not, and in all ways that we did not expect. And when He comes, all will be calm.[2]

Most of all, let us rejoice in knowing that a day is coming when this same Lord Jesus will bring all his storm-tossed disciples safely to his heavenly shore. At that time, our straining will be over, our anxiety will be ended and all our questions will be answered. And we will be at rest. Until then, let us join Edward Hopper in singing,

Jesus, Saviour, pilot me
Over life's tempestuous sea;
Unknown waves around me roll,
Hiding rocks and treach'rous shoal;
Chart and compass came from Thee;
Jesus, Saviour, pilot me.

As a mother stills her child,
Thou canst hush the ocean wild;
Boist'rous waves obey Thy will,
When Thou say'st to them, 'Be still!'
Wondrous Sov'reign of the sea,
Jesus, Saviour, pilot me.

(1871)

Reflect on these points

1. *The Lord Jesus still uses difficulties to teach and discipline his people. He always does so out of a heart of love for them and with their best interests in mind.*

2. *While we modern believers are not miracle-working apostles, we can rest assured that our Lord still supplies us with enabling grace so we can live for him.*

3. *While Simon's mastery of the water lasted just a moment, the saints' eventual mastery of all creation will last for ever.*

4. *Let us rejoice in knowing that a day is coming when this same Lord Jesus will bring all his storm-tossed disciples safely to his heavenly shore.*

The awful and
the wonderful
(Mark 9:14–29)

'Teacher, I brought You my son, who has a mute spirit. And wherever it seizes him, it throws him down; he foams at the mouth, gnashes his teeth, and becomes rigid. So I spoke to Your disciples, that they should cast it out, but they could not.'

Mark 9:17–18

Three of Jesus's disciples (Peter, James and John) had gone with him 'up on a high mountain' (v. 2). There they saw things of an absolutely astounding nature. Jesus was 'transfigured before them' (v. 2), that is, he took on a heavenly appearance. These three disciples also saw Moses and Elijah appearing with Jesus (v. 4). To top it all off, they heard the Father speak these words about Jesus from a cloud that overshadowed them: 'This is My beloved Son. Hear Him!' (v. 7).

From that mountaintop of glory, Jesus and the disciples descended to some sad realities on the plain. In trying to find help for his son, a father had amassed a large crowd and had embarrassed Jesus's disciples, who were unable to meet the need. As the father watched their vain attempts to help, his gloom must have deepened (and the glee of the scribes, who were enemies of Jesus, must have heightened). Then Jesus came, and everything was different.

As we read Mark's account of this situation, we are able to identify some awful things and some wonderful things.

Awful things (vv. 14–19)

THERE IS AN AWFUL PRESENCE HERE

Satan is not mentioned in this account, but he is definitely here. He is represented by one of the many demons who make up his evil empire. This demon had possessed the boy in a very cruel way. In addition to rendering the lad both deaf and mute, this demon delighted in flinging him to the ground, where he wallowed, foamed at the mouth, gnashed his teeth and finally became rigid. Furthermore, the demon had often sought to kill the boy by casting him into water or fire.

What a heart-wrenching situation! The poor boy! The poor father!

Many doubt the existence of the devil, but he is real. We need only look at the wreckage of bodies, minds, families, careers and happiness to be convinced of his reality. The devil is a wrecker. He wrecks people in this life and in the life to come. What the devil rules, he ruins.

THERE IS AN AWFUL ABSENCE HERE

The tyranny of the devil could be easily seen, and that was reason enough to bring sadness to the heart of Jesus. Intensifying Jesus's sadness was what he could not see: faith. He looked for faith somewhere and saw faithlessness everywhere.

No sooner did Jesus hear the father's sad account of his son's condition (vv. 17–18) than he responded with the words, 'O faithless generation, how long shall I be with you? How long shall I bear with you?' (v. 19).

To whom did Jesus direct these words? He was surrounded by

'a great multitude' (v. 14). His disciples were there. Some of the religious leaders of the Jews were there ('the scribes'—v. 16). The boy's father was there. Many, many onlookers were there, too. So who was lacking in faith? All of them! William Hendriksen says of Jesus,

> He was evidently deeply dissatisfied with his contemporaries: with the father, who lacked sufficient faith in Christ's healing power (Mark 9:22–24); with the scribes, who, instead of showing any pity, were in all probability gloating over the disciples' impotence (Mark 9:14); with the crowd in general, which is pictured in the Gospels as being generally far more concerned about itself than about others (John 6:26); and, last but not least, with the nine disciples, because of their failure to exercise their faith by putting their whole heart into persevering prayer (Mark 9:29).[1]

The Lord did not need the faith of his disciples, the scribes, the father or the spectators to drive the demon out of this boy. His power cannot be increased by faith or decreased by the lack of it. That power is constant and unchanging. But while the Lord does not need our faith, he desires it and works to create it. He does not need it, but he knows that we need it.

Wonderful things (vv. 20–29)
The awful things in this passage are truly awful, but there are wonderful things as well, things so wonderful that they overshadow the awful.

A WONDERFUL CONFESSION

After decrying the absence of faith all around him, Jesus commanded that the boy be brought to him (v. 19). As the boy was approaching Jesus, the demon possessing him sent him into a terrible convulsion (v. 20). With the boy wallowing at his feet, Jesus asked the father how long this child had been so afflicted. The Lord who had deplored the lack of faith was now creating faith in the heart of this man.

The father wanted to believe, but doubt was waging war on his faith. The doubt was there in his words to Jesus: 'if You can do anything, have compassion on us and help us' (v. 22).

What a horrible 'if'! The man suggested that Jesus might not have the power to cast out the demon. If he had only understood in whose presence he stood, he would have kept his 'if' to himself!

Jesus set the record straight in no uncertain terms. The true 'if' did not lie with him but with the father. Jesus could do the work, but could the father believe (v. 23)?

In a flash, the man realized how wrong he had been to suppose any deficiency in Jesus and he cried, 'Lord, I believe; help my unbelief!' (v. 24). It was a wonderful confession. Yes, he believed in Jesus, but his faith, while real, was still weak and needed to be strengthened.

A WONDERFUL CONQUEST

With the father's confession in place, the Lord said to the demon, 'I command you, come out of him and enter him no more!' (v. 25).

It was no mere man who issued this command but rather the Lord of glory, clothed in human flesh and invested with supreme authority. The demon, therefore, had no choice but to give up his possession, which he did after convulsing the boy one more time.

The devil's grip on this lad was broken because the devil is no match for the Lord Jesus. If the Lord could deliver this boy from a demon of hell, he can deliver us from hell itself.

A WONDERFUL CORRECTION

The nine disciples of Jesus must have rejoiced when they saw Jesus win the victory over the demon. But why had they not been able to drive that demon out? They had done it before (6:7, 13), so why not this time? Jesus gave them the answer: 'This kind can come out by nothing but prayer and fasting' (v. 29).

Was Jesus saying that they had come up against a super-demon that required more prayer and fasting than ordinary demons? Some think so. However, the phrase 'this kind' does not refer to that particular demon but rather to the whole reality of demon possession. In other words, Jesus was not saying this: 'No prayer or little prayer is fine when you are dealing with ordinary demons, but you must use super-prayer when you are dealing with a super-demon.' Instead, he was saying something of this nature: 'This kind of thing, demon possession, requires ongoing prayer and fasting. You drove out demons before because you prayed and fasted, but you did not drive this one out because you did not pray and fast.' The difference was not in the demons; it was in the disciples.

Reflect on these points

1. *The devil is a wrecker. He wrecks people in this life and in the life to come.*

2. *While the Lord does not need our faith, he desires it and works to create it. He does not need it, but he knows that we need it.*

3. *Real faith is often weak and needs to be strengthened.*

4. *If the Lord could deliver this boy from a demon of hell, he can deliver us from hell itself.*

A fish and a coin
(Matt. 17:24–27)

When they had come to Capernaum, those who received the temple tax came to Peter and said, 'Does your Teacher not pay the temple tax?' He said, 'Yes.'

Matt. 17:24–25

Jesus and his disciples had been away from Capernaum for a while. When they returned, the collectors of the temple tax approached Simon Peter to ask about Jesus paying it (v. 24).

The Jews were at this time under the heel of the Roman Empire, but this was not a Roman tax; it was a Jewish tax that every Jewish man over the age of twenty was required to pay. It was a 'ransom' tax. In paying it, each man acknowledged his debt to God and his need to be ransomed from his sins. It consisted of half a shekel for each man (Exod. 30:12–14; 38:26).

Simon Peter responded to the tax collectors' question with a simple 'Yes' (v. 25). He was confident that Jesus would pay the tax—and so Jesus did, but not as anyone would have expected!

While the miracle of this passage is not often mentioned on lists of the major miracles of Jesus, nevertheless it is one that is truly impressive and astonishing. It sets forth in a wonderful way both the glory of Jesus's person and the nature of his mission.

The glory of Jesus's person

After his talk with the tax collectors, Simon Peter went into the house where Jesus was (v. 25). We assume that he was intending to ask Jesus whether he had given the right answer about the tax. Was Jesus really going to pay it?

Divine knowledge (v. 25)

However, Simon Peter did not get to bring the matter up because Jesus mentioned it first! He knew both that Simon Peter had been talking with the tax collectors and what they had talked about. Here is supernatural knowledge. It is knowledge that no mere man or woman could possess. It is, as William Hendriksen terms it, 'penetrating knowledge'.[1]

Divine Sonship (vv. 25–26)

Jesus did not simply bring up the matter of taxes; he did so in such a way as to affirm that he was the Son of God. He asked Simon Peter, 'From whom do the kings of the earth take customs or taxes, from their sons or from strangers?' (v. 25).

The answer was obvious: kings do not tax their sons; they tax 'strangers', that is, people to whom they are not personally related. They tax their citizens in order to provide for their sons. So, as Jesus affirmed, 'the sons are free' (v. 26).

Jesus was declaring that he, the Son of God, was not obliged to pay this temple tax. The tax was collected from people for God. Since Jesus was God, he did not owe the tax!

Divine authority (v. 27)

Although Jesus fell outside the scope of the tax, he agreed to pay it—but he would not pay it as an ordinary man would. Instead, he would pay it in such a way as to demonstrate once again that he was truly God. He would not 'fish' in his pocket for the money; he would cause a fish to bring him the money! He told Simon Peter to go to the sea and cast a hook into it. He would find in the mouth of the fish that 'comes up first' a piece of money that would be sufficient to pay the taxes for both Jesus and himself (v. 27).

Isn't it interesting that Jesus did not say to Simon, 'Take the coin, and go and pay our taxes'? No, Jesus told Simon to give the tax collectors the coin 'for Me and you' (v. 27). Jesus and Simon Peter were not in the same tax bracket! Jesus was paying a debt he did not owe; Simon Peter, one that he did owe.

What a way to pay taxes! Jesus knew that the fish would be there and that the money would be there. So we have divine knowledge again! Jesus knew these things because he was able to control that fish from afar. That is divine authority!

The nature of Jesus's mission

When he was catching that fish and paying the taxes, Simon Peter probably did not realize the awesome reality that was being portrayed for him. The gospel was in those taxes, that hook and that fish! It probably only occurred to Simon Peter when he stood on the other side of the cross and looked back. Then it hit him: Jesus had come to this earth to pay a debt that he did not owe!

All the rest of us owe a tremendous debt. Because of our sinfulness, we should pay the penalty of eternal separation from God. In other words, we should endure the eternal wrath of God.

Jesus fell outside that demand. He was the perfectly holy God before he came to this world in our humanity. After he came, he was still perfect because he never sinned while he was here. So he did not have so much as a single sin to pay for. He was free! Yet he came because the God whose holy character demands the judgement of sinners is also the God who loves to show mercy to sinners.

If it is possible to speak of God having a dilemma, we can say that the salvation of sinners posed a dilemma for him. It presented him with this question: how could he both carry out the penalty that he had pronounced upon sinners and let those sinners go free? He could not merely set aside the penalty. To do so would amount to him denying or violating his justice. The dilemma was to find a way to satisfy his justice, which demanded the judgement of sinners, and also to satisfy his grace, which demanded the release of those sinners.

Jesus came to this earth as the answer to that dilemma. We will never fully appreciate his saving work until we understand that he was under no obligation to lift a finger to save us. But just as Jesus agreed to pay the temple tax he did not owe, so he agreed to pay the sin debt he did not owe! He did not have to come to this earth in our humanity, but he came. It was essential for us that he did this. In order to do something for us, he had to be one of us. In that humanity, he lived in perfect obedience to the just and holy law of God. Then he went to the cross to die a special kind of death. On the cross, he actually received the wrath of God in the stead of sinners. He did not have to do any of it, but he chose to do all of it. He voluntarily submitted to that from which he was free.

We must also note that, just as the coin in the mouth of the fish was sufficient to pay the temple tax, so Jesus's death on the cross was and is sufficient to pay for the sins of all who trust in Jesus.

The message of Christianity is this: the God of glory took our humanity to pay the sin debt of his people so they can share his glory.

Reflect on these points

1. *Jesus knew both that Simon Peter had been talking with the tax collectors and what they had talked about. Here is supernatural knowledge.*

2. *Jesus, the Son of God, was not obliged to pay this temple tax. The tax was collected from people for God. Since Jesus was God, he did not owe the tax!*

3. *Just as Jesus agreed to pay the temple tax he did not owe, so he agreed to pay the sin debt he did not owe!*

4. *Just as Jesus showed his glory in the way he paid his taxes, so he showed his glory in the way he provided salvation for sinners.*

Two men,
two meetings,
two miracles
(John 9:1–41)

Now as Jesus passed by, He saw a man who was blind from birth. And His disciples asked Him, saying, 'Rabbi, who sinned, this man or his parents, that he was born blind?' Jesus answered, 'Neither this man nor his parents sinned, but that the works of God should be revealed in him.'

John 9:1–3

This chapter records two meetings of two men—a man blind from birth and the Lord Jesus Christ. The first meeting ended in the blind man receiving sight and the second in him receiving salvation. We could say that the first meeting resulted in him receiving physical sight and the second in him receiving spiritual sight.

What wonderful meetings! We can be sure that the man never forgot either, and that he always treasured the latter more than the former.

These meetings took place in Jerusalem. Jesus was there to attend the Feast of the Tabernacles (John 7:2), which was the Jews' annual commemoration of their fathers' journeying in the wilderness during the time of Moses.

We can capture the essence of these two meetings by describing them as three movements, the first of which is …

From the puzzle to the purpose (vv. 1–5)

Jesus was walking when he came upon the blind man. Jesus had infuriated the religious leaders by claiming that he was greater than their father Abraham and that he had existed before Abraham (8:48–59). Regarding this as intolerable arrogance, the religious leaders 'took up stones to throw at Him' (8:59). How did Jesus manage to get through 'the midst of them' without a stone being hurled? His passing by may have been very near to being a miracle itself!

As Jesus 'passed by', he came upon this blind man. We must not think, however, that it was mere chance that brought Jesus and this poor man together. This meeting occurred by divine appointment.

The disciples of Jesus looked on this blind man and saw a puzzle. How was his blindness to be explained? Either the man must have sinned while he was in his mother's womb, or the parents of the man must have sinned (v. 2).

Where the disciples saw a puzzle, Jesus saw a purpose. The blindness was not to be attributed to this man's sin or to his parents' sin. The purpose of it was 'that the works of God should be revealed in him' (v. 3). This man's blindness had been designed for the very moment described in these verses— that moment when Jesus would heal him and show himself to be 'the light of the world' (v. 5).

While all suffering is due to sin, we must not connect an instance of suffering with a particular sin. Sometimes this is true, but it is not true in every case.

Was it unfair for this man to experience years of blindness so that Jesus could heal him? If we could talk to the man himself, he would say otherwise. He would tell us that he would be willing to go through it all again if in so doing he could bring glory to Jesus, who healed him of his physical blindness and rescued him from spiritual blindness.

It is interesting that Jesus quickly moved from the theological dilemma posed by this man to the work that he had come to do. He pointed out the urgency of this work ('while it is day'—v. 4). We who follow the Lord Jesus need to see that we also have work to do—work for him! There will be an eternity for us to get our questions answered, but this life offers us a very limited time to work for the Lord.

From the mud to the muddle (vv. 6–34)

Having swept away the theological puzzle posed by the disciples, Jesus proceeded to implement a very odd treatment. He made mud by spitting into the dirt, and then applied the mud to each of the man's eyes (v. 6). He then told the man to go to the pool of Siloam and wash the mud off his eyes (v. 7). John records the result of all this in these unadorned words: 'So he went and washed, and came back seeing' (v. 7).

Jesus used spit, dirt and a pool to give this man sight! There was certainly nothing in those elements that could cure blindness. The cure lay not in them but rather in Jesus who used them. Jesus could use these elements, two of which were unpleasant and insulting (the spit and dirt) and all of which were obviously inadequate, because he was and is the Lord of all natural elements and the Lord over blindness. If we were to put mud on the eyes of a blind person, we would only make him or her angry!

That mud—obviously offensive and seemingly inadequate,

yet finally effective—should make us think of Christ's death on the cross. To those who pride themselves on their wisdom, that cross continues to be offensive and inadequate in providing eternal salvation. In the plan and purpose of God, however, that cross is effective (1 Cor. 1:18–25).

Jesus's use of mud led to quite a muddle. It led to confusion! It was such confusion that John found it necessary to devote most of his account to it. The neighbours of the man wondered how he could now see. 'Those who previously had seen that he was blind' (v. 8) probably refers to people who had simply passed by on several occasions. They were uncertain about whether the man they were now seeing was the same one they had seen then.

The Pharisees were in the greatest muddle of all. Jesus had given this man sight. How could they accept that without endorsing Jesus, whom they hated? The fact that Jesus healed this man on the Sabbath gave them their opening. In making the mud, Jesus had done unnecessary work on the Sabbath: surely the man could have stayed blind one more day!

The religious leaders used three arguments to get around the evidence for the healing. They first insisted that nothing had happened (v. 18).

Desperate to find a way to get around the miracle, the Pharisees met with the man's parents. They were evidently hoping to prove either that he had not really been blind at all, or perhaps that the man who claimed to be healed was actually a seeing man who happened to look like this couple's son. They may have been imagining that Jesus had seen the resemblance and had convinced this man to claim to be 'healed'.

The Pharisees' second argument was that something had indeed happened but not what the blind man thought (v. 24). They suggested that the man had been healed, but not through the power of Jesus. God had done it for him, and Jesus, they argued, just happened to be there fiddling with his mud.

Their third argument was that no one could know for sure what had happened (v. 29).

The real problem was that these leaders had drawn their conclusion before looking at the evidence. With that conclusion firmly planted in their minds, they would not let the evidence speak for itself, but rather looked for a way to get around it. Their strategies are still used today against those who claim to have been changed by Christ.

The healed man, refusing to be swayed by the religious leaders, made three truths clear: a dramatic change had taken place (v. 25), that change had taken place at the command of Jesus (vv. 25, 30), and this change was of such a nature that it could only be explained as an act of God (v. 33).

The muddle came to an end when the Pharisees excommunicated the man from the temple (v. 34).

From exclusion to inclusion (vv. 35–41)

The exclusion of this man from the temple led to his second meeting with Jesus, who, having sought and found him, asked, 'Do you believe in the Son of God?' (v. 35).

The man responded with this question: 'Who is He, Lord,

that I may believe in Him?' (v. 36). Jesus replied, 'You have both seen Him and it is He who is talking with you' (v. 37).

That was all it took. The man said, 'Lord, I believe!' and bowed in worship before Jesus (v. 38). He had earlier expressed the opinion that Jesus was a prophet (v. 17). Now he came to the full truth about Jesus.

The excluded man had become the included man! He had been excluded from the false religion of the Pharisees but, by the grace of Christ, included in the family of God.

So a doubly blind man (blind physically and originally blind to the truth about Jesus) was now the doubly seeing man. He could see Jesus physically and he could see the truth about Jesus. All this was due not to any merit in the man himself, but to the grace of the Lord.

Meanwhile, it was the religious leaders, who assured themselves that they could see very clearly on matters of religion, who were actually blind. Their problem was not so much their blindness as their unwillingness to admit it. They were in the presence of the One who could open blind eyes. If they had admitted their blindness, the blind-healer, Jesus, would have opened their eyes. However, they were so sure that they were seeing that they remained blind (vv. 40–41).

It is obvious that Jesus intended the physical healing of this man to culminate in his spiritual healing. The one was a picture of the other. These healings yield the following conclusions about salvation:

• Just as this man was physically blind and totally unable

to help himself, so we are all by nature spiritually blind and helpless (2 Cor. 4:4).

- Just as this man was physically healed by the grace and power of Jesus, so we are spiritually healed by the same means (Eph. 2:8–9).

- Just as Jesus used seemingly inadequate and absurd means (clay, spit, the pool) to heal this man, so he uses his seemingly inadequate and apparently absurd death on the cross to provide salvation (1 Cor. 1:18–25).

- Just as this man was spiritually healed by believing in Jesus, so we are saved in the same way. What does it mean to believe in Jesus? True belief consists in knowing the facts about Jesus, believing that those facts are true, and trusting in or relying upon them for salvation. True belief always involves commitment.

- Just as this man readily obeyed Jesus's commands (v. 7) and eagerly worshipped him (v. 38), so those who are saved will desire to obey the Lord and worship Christ.

- Just as this man encountered opposition because of the change he experienced, so believers in Christ can expect opposition because of the spiritual change he has made in their lives (2 Tim. 3:12).

Reflect on these points

1. *There will be an eternity for us to get our questions answered, but this life offers us a very limited time to work for the Lord.*

2. *The mud Jesus made—so obviously offensive and seemingly inadequate, yet finally effective—should make us think of his death on the cross.*

3. *A doubly blind man (blind physically and originally blind to the truth about Jesus) became the doubly seeing man. He could see Jesus physically and he could see the truth about Jesus.*

A picture of
greater things
(Luke 17:11–19)

Now it happened as He went to Jerusalem that He passed through the midst of Samaria and Galilee. Then as He entered a certain village, there met Him ten men who were lepers, who stood afar off. And they lifted up their voices and said, 'Jesus, Master, have mercy on us!'

Luke 17:11–13

The Lord Jesus came to this earth to provide salvation for sinners. His was a saving mission. He said of himself, 'the Son of Man has come to seek and to save that which was lost' (19:10). His miracles must be interpreted in light of that saving work. They are part of it and not separate from it. Richard D. Phillips is right in his assessment that the miracles of Jesus 'inform us' of Jesus's greater work of redemption.[1]

The healing of the men in this passage is particularly helpful in setting before us Jesus's saving work. Phillips says that this miracle gives us 'an extensive view of Christian salvation'.[2] Each of the major parts of this miracle points to the greater reality of salvation.

A greater disease (vv. 11–12)

As Jesus was travelling between Galilee and Samaria, he came upon a ghastly fellowship enforced by the dreadful reality of leprosy. Jews and Samaritans did not usually associate with one another, but the ugly reality of leprosy had brought nine Jews and one Samaritan together. It gave them a common bond that transcended everything else. If someone had leprosy, it did not matter that he or she was a Jew or a Samaritan. Such a person was a leper! Not a Jewish leper or a Samaritan leper—just a leper!

Leprosy is a disease whose symptoms include white patches on the skin, running sores and the eating away of the flesh. In biblical times, lepers were required to stay away from others. They were unclean, as was anyone who touched them. It was not uncommon in those days for lepers to band together and to cry out, 'Unclean! Unclean!' as others came near.

Leprosy made those who contracted it more dead than alive. It was something of a living death.

Why is there such a disease as leprosy? The Bible gives us the answer. It tells us that this world is not as God made it. Everything that is wrong in this world is due to sin. Sin is the universal malady. We all come into this world with a sinful nature that leads us always to sinful acts. Sin is its own kind of living death. It causes us to be dead spiritually even while we are alive physically. It causes us to be unclean in the sight of the God who is infinitely holy.

The leprosy of this passage pictures, then, the greater disease of sin. But also pictured here is …

A greater deliverance (vv. 13–14)

When these ten lepers saw Jesus, they recognized him. Apparently, some of their number had seen and heard him before they became lepers. They may very well have seen him perform various miracles, including the healing of lepers (Matt. 11:5; Mark 1:40–42). So the sight of him did not prompt them to offer their usual cry of 'Unclean! Unclean!'; this time they 'lifted up their voices' to cry, 'Jesus, Master, have mercy on us!' (v. 13).

The ten lepers had now become a choir, uniting their voices in an anthem pleading for mercy. No cry so targets the heart of the Lord and nothing so wins it as the cry for mercy. The Lord loves mercy. He delights in it.

Jesus's response to their plea may appear to some to be a bit surprising. He did not tell them that they were healed but rather said, 'Go, show yourselves to the priests' (v. 14).

On this occasion, the Lord wanted to show that he channels his mercy through faith. Would these men now believe his Word and do what he commanded? Jesus was requiring them to go to the priests who alone could pronounce them clean while they were still unclean. He was requiring them to go with their blotches and splotches, their oozing sores and their rotting flesh.

The lepers could have looked at one another and said, 'There's no need to go to the priests. We still have our leprosy.' But they obeyed the command of Jesus and set out. The cleansing for which they had pleaded took place while they were on their way (v. 14). Ten men had been delivered from the horror of leprosy by the grace and power of the Lord Jesus Christ!

Their deliverance, amazing as it was, cannot begin to compare to one far greater, namely, the deliverance Jesus grants to sinners. Jesus saves sinners when they come to him in the foulness of their sins and plead for his mercy. But we must come to him in our sins, just as the lepers started walking towards the priests while they were still lepers. Joseph Hart states this truth in these memorable lines:

> Come, ye sinners, poor and needy,
> Weak and wounded, sick and sore;
> Jesus ready stands to save you,
> Full of pity, love and pow'r.
>
> Let not conscience make you linger,
> Nor of fitness fondly dream;
> All the fitness He requireth
> Is to feel your need of Him.
>
> Come, ye weary, heavy-laden,
> Lost and ruined by the fall;
> If you tarry till you're better,
> You will never come at all.
>
> (1759)

Those who come to Christ in the guilt of their sins will find forgiveness. Just as the lepers stood in the presence of the priests and were pronounced clean, so those who trust in Christ are pronounced clean by the God who is the Judge of all the earth.

A greater debt (vv. 15–19)

As we have noted, the ten lepers were cleansed in the act of going to the priests. Nine continued their journey, but one, realizing fully the immense debt that he owed Jesus, turned back to fall at his feet to give him thanks (v. 16).

Because the Jewish nation had for centuries been so rich in spiritual privileges, we might expect that some of the nine Jews gave thanks to the Lord. But the thanks came from the one who had not enjoyed such privileges.

Why did the nine not join the one in giving thanks? Perhaps they thought it was possible to be thankful without openly expressing it!

It is very easy for us to be critical of those nine men, all of whom richly deserve criticism. But are we any better than they? Because sin is a greater disease than leprosy, salvation from sin is a greater deliverance. If salvation is a greater deliverance, it imposes upon us a greater debt—the debt of gratitude! Robert Robinson conveys this in these words:

> Oh, to grace how great a debtor
> Daily I'm constrained to be!
> Let Thy goodness, like a fetter,
> Bind my wand'ring heart to Thee.
>
> ('Come, Thou Fount of Every Blessing', 1757)

Do we daily feel our debt to the Lord's grace? Are we giving thanks daily? Are our thanks heartfelt, or are they mechanical and stilted? Do we attend public worship as we should? Do we genuinely praise God while we are in public worship? Do we pray? Do we remember to include thanksgiving in our prayers? Do we reserve our highest praise for salvation? Do we support the Lord's work by generously giving our money? Do we minister in the Lord's name? Are we truly thankful?

In Luke 7:36–50, we read about a woman who wept with gratitude at the feet of Jesus until her tears covered his feet. She then dried his feet with her hair. This woman was grateful to Jesus because he had forgiven her. She powerfully shows us two things: we won't love Christ if we don't know forgiveness, and we won't know forgiveness if we don't know our sinfulness.

Alexander Maclaren asks this question: 'Why is it that such multitudes of you professing Christians are such icebergs in your Christianity?'[3] He answers his question by saying, 'Mainly for this reason—that you have never found out in anything like an adequate measure, how great a sinner you are, and how sure and sweet and sufficient Christ's pardoning mercy is.'[4]

Christianity can be summarized in three words: guilt, grace and gratitude. If we have known the guilt and grace, there will be gratitude. Gratitude is, of course, a matter of degrees. Every Christian will have some of it and will desire to have more of it.

We tend to think that the most blessed are the most thankful. The Samaritan leper learned, however, that the most thankful are the most blessed. After he gave thanks, the Lord Jesus said, 'Arise, go your way. You faith has made you well' (v. 19).

The man was not saved by his gratitude, but he was given reassurance of his salvation because of his gratitude. The Christians who are the most thankful for their salvation will also be the most assured that they are saved, and that will serve to increase their gratitude.

Reflect on these points

1. *Everything that is wrong in this world is due to sin. Sin is the universal malady.*

2. *No cry so targets the heart of the Lord and nothing so wins it as the cry for mercy.*

3. *Jesus saves sinners when they come to him in the foulness of their sins and plead for his mercy.*

4. *Because sin is a greater disease than leprosy, salvation from sin is a greater deliverance. If salvation is a greater deliverance, it imposes upon us a greater debt—the debt of gratitude!*

5. *Christianity can be summarized in three words: guilt, grace and gratitude. If we have known the guilt and grace, there will be gratitude.*

The king of terrors yields to the King of kings
(John 11:1–47)

Now a certain man was sick, Lazarus of Bethany, the town of Mary and her sister Martha. It was that Mary who anointed the Lord with fragrant oil and wiped His feet with her hair, whose brother Lazarus was sick. Therefore the sisters sent to Him, saying, 'Lord, behold, he whom You love is sick.'

John 11:1–3

This passage begins with mystery and ends in majesty. The mystery is found in Jesus's refusal to go to the village of Bethany when he heard that his dear friend Lazarus was sick. Jesus stayed away and Lazarus died. The majesty is found in Jesus raising Lazarus from the dead. Jesus created the mystery so he could reveal the majesty. Lazarus had to die so that 'the Son of God [might] be glorified' (v. 4).

The blind man's blindness, recounted earlier in John, was designed for the glory of God (9:3), and so was Lazarus's death. We fret over these things now, but when God fully reveals his glory in eternity, we will see their rightness.

Death is the king of terrors. Nothing so strikes fear into the human heart as death. Death can cause even the bravest and most heroic to become whimpering cowards.

Death has conducted its reign of terror from the moment when Adam and Eve brought sin into this world and turned the Garden of Eden into the Garden of Evil. Death's reign is expressed in three forms: physical death, the separation of the soul from the body; spiritual death, the separation of the soul from God; and eternal death, the separation of body and soul from God for ever.

The good news trumpeted by this account of Lazarus is that there is One greater than death. Jesus is the King of kings, and the king of terrors is no match for him.

So Jesus went to Bethany to engage the rival king in combat and to win him over. John lays it all out for us in careful detail. To our considerable surprise, however, he is the only Gospel writer to record this miracle. It was of such an astounding nature that it would seem fitting for it to be in each of the Gospels. Here is another mystery that will only be cleared up in the presence of the Lord of Glory.

John's account emphasizes the special nature of this miracle. Jesus had raised dead people previously (the widow's son and Jairus's daughter), but the raising of Lazarus was in a class all its own. It was special for at least three reasons:

It was performed in a situation that appeared to be beyond impossible

John lays stress on the fact that Lazarus had already been dead four days when Jesus arrived on the scene (vv. 17, 39). What is the significance of the four days?

The Jews believed that, after death, the spirit of the person hovered over the body for three days to see if it was going to come back to life so it could be re-inhabited. On the fourth day, the spirit withdrew. To the Jewish mind, then, the four-day dead person was beyond all hope. The situation was then irreversible.

Martha and Mary, the sisters of Lazarus, struggled to have faith in Jesus. They wanted so much to believe that Jesus could and would raise Lazarus, but the fact that he had been dead so long seemed to make such belief utter folly. We have no trouble hearing the despair in Martha's words to Jesus: 'Lord, by this time there is a stench, for he has been dead four days' (v. 39).

Martha could have entertained the possibility of a resurrection if Jesus had arrived during the pre-stench stage, but now they were in the post-stench stage. While Martha struggled to believe, unbelief perched on her shoulder and whispered in her ear, 'Decay has set in and there is no hope!'

Martha failed to understand fully that Jesus, the God-Man, is the possessor of supernatural power and, therefore, there is no reason to put any kind of limitation on that power. God's power is just as sufficient post-stench as it is pre-stench!

Jesus would later make that very point in a powerful way when the Sadducees, the resurrection sceptics of the day, put one of their 'resurrection riddles' before him (Mark 12:18–27). Their riddle was designed to put the thought of resurrection into a realm of such complexity that any possibility of it had to be ruled out. Jesus blew their riddle out of the water by simply observing that the Sadducees had never really reckoned with the power of God (Mark 12:24). With God there are no such things as 'possible' resurrections and 'impossible' resurrections. Nothing is too hard for him!

It was performed in a particularly gripping way
Three things stand out about the way in which Jesus performed this miracle. One is that ...

HE ANNOUNCED IT IN ADVANCE

When Jesus arrived in Bethany, Martha went to meet him while Mary remained in the house (v. 20). Jesus immediately assured Martha that Lazarus would rise again. Martha took that as a reference to the resurrection 'at the last day' (v. 24).

Jesus responded with some of the most comforting and blessed words in the Bible: 'I am the resurrection and the life. He who believes in Me, though he may die, he shall live. And whoever lives and believes in Me shall never die' (vv. 25–26). Jesus was essentially telling Martha that there was no need to be thinking of the resurrection of the last day while he, the resurrection and the life, was standing right in front of her.

The second factor that stands out about this miracle is that …

HE ACCOMPLISHED IT WITH ONLY THREE WORDS

After consoling Martha and Mary, and after registering his outrage over the havoc sin has caused in this world (yes, the phrases 'groaned in the spirit' and 'was troubled', v. 33, are to be understood as indicating the utter revulsion he felt towards the ugliness of sin and the damage it creates), Jesus came to the tomb. There he commanded that the stone covering the mouth of the tomb be removed (v. 39) and he communed with the Father (vv. 41–42).

Then it happened! With a loud voice, he cried, 'Lazarus, come forth!' (v. 43)—and Lazarus 'came out' (v. 44)! With three words, Jesus offset four days!

The third aspect that stands out about the way Jesus performed this miracle is that …

HIS WORDS CARRIED LAZARUS OUT OF THE GRAVE

We should not picture Lazarus walking out of the tomb in response to Jesus's cry. The fact that he was still 'bound hand and foot' (v. 44) when he came out indicates that the power of the Lord Jesus carried him out of that tomb.

It was performed before many witnesses

We can be sure that Jesus's loud cry was not given for the sake of Lazarus. The power of Jesus is such that Lazarus could have heard a whisper. It was rather for the sake of all those who were nearby. Jesus wanted them to know what was taking place. His loud cry inextricably connected Lazarus's resurrection with his words. That cry was intended to create many witnesses.

How many witnessed this miracle? John does not give us a number. He does tell us that 'many of the Jews had joined the women around Martha and Mary, to comfort them concerning their brother' (v. 19). We must remember that when John uses the phrase 'the Jews', he is not referring to the populace in general but rather to the religious leaders of Jerusalem. After Lazarus came out of the tomb, 'many of the Jews' believed in Jesus (v. 45).

Others refused to believe and went to the Pharisees to report what had happened (v. 46). This led to a meeting of religious leaders for the purpose of determining what should be done with Jesus (v. 47). It is very significant that these men made no attempt to deny the miracle. Something so well attested could not be successfully disputed!

The king of terrors, death, had laid hold of Lazarus, but the King of kings forced him to let Lazarus go. So now there should be no doubt that Jesus is indeed the King of kings. When we later read that Jesus arose from the grave, we should say, 'Of course he did! How could it be otherwise? The One who can raise the dead is Lord over death, and the Lord over death must himself be raised from the dead!'

There should be no doubt that the One who raised Lazarus was and is God. Since God cannot lie, there should be no doubt that he will keep his promise eventually to raise all the dead. There should also be no doubt that not all resurrections will be the same. Those who know Christ will be raised to experience eternal life; those who do not know him, to experience eternal condemnation (5:28–29). As always, then, the greatest business of life is to make sure we know Christ by repenting of our sins and trusting him and him alone as the Saviour for sinners. Only those who believe in Jesus 'shall live' (11:25).

Reflect on these points

1. *There is One greater than death. Jesus is the King of kings, and the king of terrors is no match for him.*

2. *With God there are no such things as 'possible' resurrections and 'impossible' resurrections. Nothing is too hard for him!*

3. *The One who can raise the dead is Lord over death, and the Lord over death must himself be raised from the dead!*

4. *Those who know Christ will be raised to experience eternal life; those who do not know him, to experience eternal condemnation (5:28–29).*

The greatest of all miracles: Jesus
(John 1:14;
2 Corinthians 5:21;
1 Peter 3:18)

For He made Him who knew no sin to be sin for us, that we might become the righteousness of God in Him.

2 Cor. 5:21

The greatest of all miracles is the Lord Jesus himself. All the miracles of the Bible (except those performed through Satanic power) were designed to point to him.

The miracle of Jesus is threefold: his incarnation, his death and his resurrection. The texts listed at the head of this chapter set forth the miracle of Jesus being made flesh (John 1:14), made sin (2 Cor. 5:21) and made alive (1 Peter 3:18).

First, there is …

The miracle of his incarnation

The word 'incarnation' comes from a Latin word that means 'in flesh'. When we speak about the incarnation of Christ, we are referring to him taking our humanity. We must be very clear on this: in taking our humanity, Jesus did not divest himself of deity; he added to his deity our humanity. So he was fully God and fully man. The apostle John puts it perfectly when he says of Jesus, 'And the Word became flesh and dwelt among us, and we beheld His glory, the glory as of the only begotten of the Father, full of grace and truth' (John 1:14).

Yes, Jesus was flesh, but he was more—much more! John and the other disciples could see in Jesus the glory of God because he was God. Jesus himself claimed as much in these words: 'He who has seen Me has seen the Father' (John 14:9).

This is the central miracle of the Bible. C. S. Lewis calls it

'The Grand Miracle'. Concerning it, Lewis writes, 'The central miracle asserted by Christians is the Incarnation. They say that God became Man. Every other miracle prepares for this, or exhibits this, or results from this.'[1] After quoting these words from Lewis and noting the anti-supernaturalism of many of Lewis's contemporaries, Richard D. Phillips writes,

> People today are open to the supernatural, indeed to supernatural forces of all kinds. The problem today is not that no once accepts the miraculous. Far from it! Our problem is that the miracles we believe are without any meaning or purpose outside of their individual benefits. They are 'random acts of kindness' on the part of some benevolent but impersonal force in the universe.[2]

Phillips then adds,

> In contrast, the miracles of the Bible, and especially in the Gospel narratives, are inherently purposeful. The miracles of the Bible have meaning because they are tied to that grand miracle of which Lewis spoke: the coming of Jesus Christ. Our chief purpose in studying the miracles of Jesus is to study him ...[3]

The incarnation of Jesus is such a staggering thing that men and women would not have believed it had Jesus not done things that only God could do. We might say that the incarnation of Jesus is the miracle that demanded all the other miracles. The miracle of Jesus demanded that Jesus do miracles. Benjamin

Warfield puts it in a wonderful way: 'When our Lord came down to earth He drew heaven with Him. The signs which accompanied His ministry were but the trailing clouds of glory which He brought from heaven which is His home.'[4]

The second part of the miracle of Jesus is ...

The miracle of his death

So many these days do not understand the death of Jesus on the cross. When they think of it (and most seldom do), they think only in terms of a physical death. Some think about the death of Jesus to a sufficient degree to wonder about it. They have heard all their lives that Jesus died so that sinners can be forgiven their sins, but they wonder how the death of Jesus could accomplish this. The fact is that many men died on Roman crosses in those days.

If we think of the death of Jesus only as a physical death, we may very well wonder what there was about his death that set it apart from the deaths of other crucified men. Why should we look to the crucifixion of Jesus for forgiveness of our sins instead of to any other crucified man?

The answer is that we must not think of the death of Jesus in physical terms alone. Yes, Jesus, as a real man, died physically—but Jesus was more than a man. He was, as noted above, God in human flesh. The miracle of the death of Jesus lies in the special nature of that death, and its special nature lies in the transaction that took place between God the Father and God the Son while the latter was on the cross.

Before the Lord Jesus ever stepped into human history, he

entered into a covenant with God the Father. For his part, the Father agreed to accept his Son as the substitute for sinners and to pour out his wrath on his Son instead of on those sinners. God's justice demanded that God pour out his wrath on sinners.

For his part, the Son agreed to be the substitute for sinners. In other words, he agreed to receive the wrath of God in their stead. This is the miracle of the cross: in the space of the six hours Jesus was on the cross, he received an eternity's worth of the wrath of God for those he came to save!

Once we understand the special nature of what Jesus did on the cross, we will join Stuart Townend in singing,

> How deep the Father's love for us,
> How vast beyond all measure
> That He should give His only Son
> To make a wretch His treasure
> How great the pain of searing loss,
> The Father turns His face away
> As wounds which mar the chosen One,
> Bring many sons to glory
>
> Behold the Man upon a cross,
> My sin upon His shoulders
> Ashamed I hear my mocking voice
> Call out among the scoffers
> It was my sin that left Him there
> Until it was accomplished
> His dying breath has brought me life
> I know that it is finished.

The final part of the miracle of Jesus is:

The miracle of his resurrection

The miracle of the incarnation led to the miracle of the cross, and the miracle of the cross led to the miracle of the resurrection.

It was essential that Jesus die the special kind of death upon which he and the Father had agreed. It was essential for him to receive the penalty for those sinners who would believe on him so that there would be no penalty left for them.

But as vital as the cross was, it would have been to no avail if Jesus's body had rotted away in the tomb. His resurrection was also vital. It proved him to be God in human flesh and, in doing so, proved that his death on the cross was of infinite value. It also proved that God was entirely satisfied with the death of Christ in the place of sinners. God is the One we have offended through our sins, and it is God who must be satisfied. The fact that God is the One who raised Jesus from the dead proves that God was satisfied with his redeeming death.

In one sense, the cross was the verdict of sinful men on Jesus. By nailing him there, they were pronouncing him to be a fraud. The resurrection was the verdict of God on Jesus, and what a radically different verdict it was! God was reversing or setting aside the verdict of sinful men on his Son and pronouncing his own verdict on him. By raising Jesus from the dead, God was setting the record straight.

There can be no doubt that the resurrection of Jesus was a miracle. Mere men and women do not spring from their graves. Death is such a powerful reality that we are helpless before it. The resurrection of Jesus, however, broke the grip of death. There is no better word to describe his resurrection than 'miracle'.

Perhaps you are thinking along these lines: 'I wish I could believe that Jesus rose again.' You can and you must believe it! The resurrection of Jesus is not just the fanciful imaginings of men: it is based on solid evidence. The stone of his tomb was rolled away. The tomb was empty. Those appointed to guard the tomb were in a stupor. Angels were present. The grave-clothes of Jesus were left behind in a particularly convincing configuration. Many saw the risen Lord (500 on one occasion!). The disciples were transformed from cowering wimps into bold evangelists. The resurrection of Jesus is so abundantly supported by evidence that no one need be in any doubt about it.

The incarnation, death and resurrection come together to make up the miracle of Jesus. The miracles he did were not performed to call attention to themselves but rather to him, and to do so in such a way that we will break with our sins and receive him as our Lord and Saviour. Those who embrace the Jesus of the miracles will personally meet the miracle of Jesus in eternity. There in his presence they will be lost in wonder, love and praise.

Reflect on these points

1. In the taking of our humanity, Jesus did not divest himself of deity: he added to his deity our humanity. So he was fully God and fully man.

2. The incarnation of Jesus is such a staggering thing that men and women would not have believed it had Jesus not done things that only God could do.

3. The miracle of the death of Jesus lies in the special nature of that death, and its special nature lies in the transaction that took place between God the Father and God the Son while the latter was on the cross.

4. The fact that God is the One who raised Jesus from the dead proves that God was satisfied with his redeeming death.

Mighty to save

The Spirit of the Lord is upon Me, because He has anointed Me to preach the gospel to the poor; He has sent Me to heal the brokenhearted, to proclaim liberty to the captives and recovery of sight to the blind, to set at liberty those who are oppressed; to proclaim the acceptable year of the Lord.

Luke 4:18–19

Jesus did not perform his miraculous works haphazardly and randomly. Everything he did was very precise and purposeful, and the aim in all his miracles was to point to the saving work he came to this earth to perform. We might say that the miracles unite their individual voices into one, and with that one voice they cry, 'Jesus saves!'

Jesus's saving work consists of two major aspects: releasing individuals from the curse of sin and releasing the natural order from that same curse. The miracles of Jesus picture either one or the other of these aspects.

The salvation of the sinner

As we have seen, in the course of his ministry the Lord Jesus delivered people who were paralysed, lame, blind, deaf, mute, leprous, demon-possessed or dead. Each of these realities finds a spiritual parallel in the sinner. Each speaks eloquently about some aspect of the sinner's condition:

- Sinners are paralysed by their sin: left to themselves, they cannot move away from sin and towards God. They are completely incapacitated by their sin.
- Sinners are by nature spiritually lame: if being saved is a

145

matter of getting up and walking towards God, sinners cannot take so much as a single step.

- Sinners are spiritually blind: they cannot see the reality of their sin, the condemnation that their sin deserves, the judgement that is to come or the way of salvation that God has provided in Christ. It is all hidden to them.
- Sinners are spiritually deaf: they cannot hear the saving truth in the gospel. Even if they are hearing words about the gospel, those words mean nothing to them: they cannot comprehend or appreciate them.
- Sinners are spiritually mute: they cannot open their mouths to offer true praise to the God who made them and the God from whom they receive life and breath.
- Sinners are spiritually leprous: they are unclean before God.
- Sinners are spiritually the property of the devil: they are part of the devil's dark domain.
- Sinners are spiritually dead: they are not capable of feeling anything about God or of taking any spiritual action. As far as spiritual things are concerned, sinners cannot hear, think, believe, feel, love, taste, speak, sing, act or move.

Jesus chose to perform miracles that would drive home in a powerful way the terrible condition of sinners and his power to save them. By his perfect life and his redeeming death, Jesus has done everything necessary for sinners to be saved. He has made the provision. The Holy Spirit, the gift of the risen and ascended Christ, is in the business of applying to individual sinners the saving benefits secured by Christ. The Holy Spirit regenerates sinners: he makes them alive. Then sinners can truly hear, see and believe the truth. They can move towards God in genuine repentance. They can love and appreciate the things of God. They can dance with sheer joy that God has shown them mercy and that they no longer belong to the devil but to God.

William T. Matson gathered up some of these truths in these lines:

> Lord, I was blind: I could not see
> In Thy marred visage any grace;
> But now the beauty of Thy face
> In radiant vision dawns on me.
>
> Lord, I was deaf: I could not hear
> The thrilling music of Thy voice;
> But now I hear Thee and rejoice,
> And all Thine uttered words are dear.
>
> Lord, I was dumb: I could not speak
> The grace and glory of Thy Name;
> But now, as touched with living flame,
> My lips Thine eager praises wake.
>
> Lord, I was dead: I could not stir
> My lifeless soul to come to Thee;
> But now, since Thou hast quickened me,
> I rise from sin's dark sepulchre.

Lord, Thou hast made the blind to see,
The deaf to hear, the dumb to speak,
The dead to live; and lo, I break
The chains of my captivity.

(1833–1899)

The restoration of the natural order

In addition to these miracles relieving individuals of various kinds of sufferings, Jesus performed what we might call 'nature miracles'. He changed water into wine, fed multitudes, stilled storms, walked on water, filled nets with fish and paid a tax by getting a coin from the mouth of a fish.

These miracles demonstrate Jesus's authority over nature, and he will eventually use that authority to put nature back to where it was before sin entered.

Nature is not today as it was when God did his work of creation. The sin of Adam had catastrophic results for nature; no part of nature was left untouched by it. Rivers, trees, soil, animals, seas and oceans were all affected. We may find ourselves wondering why God allowed nature to suffer for Adam's sin. Why did he not cause Adam and Eve alone to suffer for it? It may be that by allowing sin to affect all of nature, God was putting all around Adam and Eve and their descendants a visible reminder of the devastating results of sin. By allowing nature to suffer, God was registering in a visible way the enormity of human sin.

The essence of redemption is to put things back to where they were. God designed the redemption of sinners in such a way to put them back to where Adam and Eve were before they sinned and, yes, even to carry those sinners beyond where Adam and Eve were in their perfect state. Isaac Watts beautifully writes of Christ,

> In him the tribes of Adam boast
> More blessings than their father lost.
>
> ('Jesus Shall Reign Where'er the Sun', 1719)

For God's work of redemption to be complete, all of creation must also be put back to where it was before sin entered. Anything less would amount to a defeat for God.

So a marvellous day is coming when creation, which is now groaning because of man's sin (Rom. 8:22), will be redeemed. It will ultimately be freed from the ravages of sin. In the same hymn, Isaac Watts writes of the Lord Jesus,

> Where he displays his healing power
> Death and the curse are known no more.

Some seem to have the idea that the final state for Christians is heaven up in the sky somewhere. That is not what the Bible teaches. The apostle John tells us that one day there will be 'a new earth' (Rev. 21:1). On that day, the words of the apostle Paul will be gloriously fulfilled: 'the creation itself also will be delivered from the bondage of corruption into the glorious liberty of the children of God' (Rom. 8:21).

The new earth is going to be indescribably wonderful. When the children of God are introduced to it, they will feel the full force of these words: 'Eye has not seen, nor ear heard, nor have entered into the heart of man the things which God has prepared for those who love Him' (1 Cor. 2:9).

So Jesus demonstrated his authority over nature in his public ministry to show that he has the power to give his people a new earth, and to give them a foretaste and guarantee of it.

We should not forget that Jesus performed one nature miracle that conveys a most solemn truth indeed. He pronounced a curse upon a fruitless fig tree, and that tree immediately withered (Matt. 21:18–19; Mark 11:12–14, 20–21). There is a sharp message in that tree. God put each of us here to be fruitful for him by living for the glory of his name. To refuse to live for the glory of God is the very essence of sin (Rom. 3:23). It is rejecting God's purpose for our lives and living for ourselves.

If we go through life in this way, we will bring God's curse upon us and will have no part in the new earth. The business of this earth is to make sure we become citizens of the new earth, and we become citizens of the new earth only through repenting of our sins and trusting in the Lord Jesus Christ.

Reflect on these points

1. *Jesus chose to perform miracles that would drive home in a powerful way the terrible condition of sinners and his power to save them.*

2. *God designed the redemption of sinners in such a way to put them back to where Adam and Eve were before they sinned and, yes, even to carry those sinners beyond where Adam and Eve were in their perfect state.*

3. *The apostle John tells us that one day there will be 'a new earth' (Rev. 21:1). On that day, the words of the apostle Paul will be gloriously fulfilled: 'the creation itself also will be delivered from the bondage of corruption into the glorious liberty of the children of God' (Rom. 8:21).*

4. *God put each of us here to be fruitful for him by living for the glory of his name. To refuse to live for the glory of God is the very essence of sin, and if we go through life in this way, we will bring God's curse upon us and will have no part in the new earth.*

Endnotes

Ch. 1 A glimpse of his glory (John 2:1–11)

1 William Hendriksen, *John* (New Testament Commentary; Grand Rapids, MI: Baker, 1953), p. 113.

2 Anthony T. Selvaggio, *The Seven Signs* (Grand Rapids, MI: Reformation Heritage Books, 2009), p. 18.

3 J. C. Ryle, *Expository Thoughts on John,* vol. i (Edinburgh: Banner of Truth, 1987), p. 102.

4 Warren Wiersbe, *The Bible Exposition Commentary,* vol. i (Wheaton, IL: Victor Books), p. 292.

5 Ryle, *Expository Thoughts on John,* p. 94.

Ch. 2 A wonder from afar (John 4:46–54)

1 William Hendriksen, *John* (New Testament Commentary; Grand Rapids, MI: Baker, 1953), p. 181.

2 Dale Ralph Davis, *1 Samuel: Looking on the Heart,* vol. i (Grand Rapids, MI: Baker, 1994), p. 53.

3 Anthony T. Selvaggio, *The Seven Signs* (Grand Rapids, MI: Reformation Heritage Books, 2009), p. 47.

4 Cited by Selvaggio, *The Seven Signs,* pp. 47–48.

5 Ibid., p. 49.

Ch. 5 The lame man and the God-Man (John 5:1–15)

1 J. C. Ryle, *Expository Thoughts on John,* vol. i (Edinburgh: Banner of Truth, 1987), p.267.

Ch. 6 Snapshots taken on the way to the cemetery (Luke 7:11–17)

1 S. G. DeGraaf, *Promise and Deliverance,* vol. iii (St Catharine's, Ontario: Paideia Press, 1979), pp. 361–362.

2 Alexander Maclaren, *Expositions of Holy Scripture,* vol. ix (Grand Rapids, MI: Baker, 1974), p. 155.

Ch. 7 The wonder of Jesus (Mark 4:35–41)

1 Charles R. Erdman, *The Gospel of Mark* (Philadelphia, PA: Westminster Press, 1917), p. 77.

Ch. 12 A string of wonders (Matt. 14:22–33; Mark 6:45–52; John 6:15–21)

1 William Hendriksen, *John* (New Testament Commentary; Grand Rapids, MI: Baker, 1953), p. 227.

2 J. C. Ryle, *Expository Thoughts on John,* vol. i (Edinburgh: Banner of Truth, 1987), p. 340.

Ch. 13 The awful and the wonderful (Mark 9:14–29)

1 William Hendriksen, *Matthew* (New Testament Commentary; Grand Rapids, MI: Baker, 1973), p. 674.

Ch. 14 A fish and a coin (Matt. 17:24–27)

1 William Hendriksen, *Matthew* (New Testament Commentary; Grand Rapids, MI: Baker, 1973), p. 679.

Ch. 16 A picture of greater things (Luke 17:11–19)

1 Richard D. Phillips, *Mighty to Save* (Phillipsburg, NJ: P&R, 2001), p. ix.

2 Ibid., p. 190.

3 Alexander Maclaren, *Expositions of Holy Scripture,* vol. ix (Grand Rapids, MI: Baker, 1974), p. 197.

4 Ibid.

Ch. 18 The greatest of all miracles: Jesus (John 1:14; 2 Corinthians 5:21; 1 Peter 3:18)

1 Quoted in Richard D. Phillips, *Mighty to Save* (Phillipsburg, NJ: P&R, 2001), p. 2.

2 Ibid., p. 3.

3 Ibid.

4 Benjamin B. Warfield, *Counterfeit Miracles* (Edinburgh: Banner of Truth, 1972), p. 3.

Also available

God's good news in the parables of Jesus

ROGER ELLSWORTH

160PP, PAPERBACK

ISBN 978-1-84625-408-6

A father's rebellious son leaves home. A man discovers treasure hidden in a field. A woman pesters a judge until he is willing to hear her case. A farmer frets over storing his crop. Drawing from the common experiences of his hearers, Jesus told these and other stories in such riveting fashion that he easily commanded a hearing. But as this book shows, he had a higher purpose than merely to captivate his audiences. These parables were designed to move them from the everyday world to the eternal world and to present them with this good news: that all who truly receive Jesus as Lord and Saviour will live with him in eternal glory.

'In brief compass Roger Ellsworth provides clear, sound exposition and application of the parables of Jesus. This volume will be very helpful to pastors and laypeople as they study the Gospels.'
RAY VAN NESTE, PROFESSOR OF BIBLICAL STUDIES AND DIRECTOR, R. C. RYAN CENTER FOR BIBLICAL STUDIES, JACKSON, TN, USA

'Pastoral wisdom and personal warmth are hallmarks of Roger Ellsworth's commentaries. Reading *God's Good News in the Parables of Jesus* and reflecting on the various points raised will no doubt encourage greater appreciation of the parables and greater love for Christ.'
BARRY KING, GENERAL SECRETARY, GRACE BAPTIST PARTNERSHIP, LONDON

They echoed the voice of God

Reflections on the Minor Prophets

ROGER ELLSWORTH

128PP, PAPERBACK

ISBN 978-1-84625-101-6

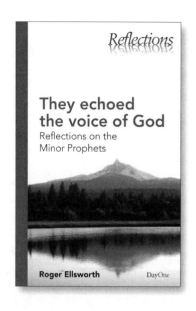

Many carry a little Bible and believe in a little God. Their Bibles are little because they ignore so many of its books. Their God is little because they ignore so many of the Bible's truths. The Minor Prophets can help us. These men made sense of their circumstances and found strength for their challenges by basking in the God who was above it all and in it all. The God they served was wise enough to plan and strong enough to achieve. This study of their messages will help us have both bigger Bibles and a bigger God.

'Roger Ellsworth helps us appreciate how the so-called Minor Prophets make known the character and work of our great God. This book is a great introduction to and overview of their prophecies. Read it to become acquainted with these sometimes overlooked servants and, more importantly, with the unchangeable God whose message they proclaimed.'
TOM ASCOL, DIRECTOR OF FOUNDERS MINISTRIES AND PASTOR, GRACE BAPTIST CHURCH, CAPE CORAL, FLORIDA

'Laced with helpful, practical application, this book shows how each prophet emphasized a particular aspect of God's character, giving an overall picture that is compelling.'
JIM WINTER, MINISTER OF HORSELL EVANGELICAL CHURCH, WOKING

When God makes streams in the desert

Revival blessings in the Bible

ROGER ELLSWORTH

128PP, PAPERBACK

ISBN 978-1-84625-176-4

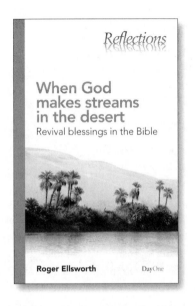

What is biblical revival? Many Christians associate revival with special meetings that used to take place once or twice a year. Guest preachers and singers would be brought in, and special evening services were designed to encourage believers to get closer to the Lord and to convince unbelievers to accept him as their Saviour.

But that is not revival. Biblical revival is about God bringing his people back to spiritual vitality. Only Christians can be revived because only they have spiritual life, having been regenerated by the Spirit of God on the basis of the redeeming work of Christ.

Learn what the Bible teaches about revival, and be inspired to pray that, even in our day, God will make streams flow in the desert!

'With a relentless focus on the Bible itself, Roger Ellsworth reminds us that true revival is a sovereign work of God that radically affects our lives. The best recommendation I can give of this book is that it made me long more intensely and pray more fervently for God to act in the midst of his people.'
CHAD DAVIS, PASTOR, GRACE COMMUNITY CHURCH, MARTIN, TENNESSEE, USA

'When God Makes Streams in the Desert reminds us that revival is present when, as Brian Edwards says, 'remarkable life and power that cannot be explained adequately in any human terms' moves into our churches and causes us to do what we do 'at a different level'. This book will change the way you think about and pray for revival.'
PAUL ORRICK, PASTOR, FIRST BAPTIST CHURCH, GREENVILLE, OHIO, USA

Hints and signs of the coming King

Pictures of Jesus in the Old Testament

KURT STRASSNER

112PP, PAPERBACK

ISBN978-1-84625-208-2

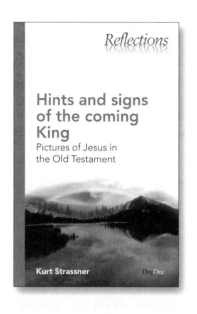

In the Bible, God often paints spiritual concepts with the bright colors of illustration: "Behold, the Lamb of God who takes away the sin of the world" (John 1:29). But it is not just Bible teaching that can be metaphoric; Bible events can be, too. God often worked out Bible history—real events, objects, and people—to show portraits of the greatest of all subjects—his beloved Son. This book examines eight such Old Testament pictures and demonstrates how they point us forward to Jesus Christ, the coming King.

'This book is an excellent evangelistic tool, particularly because it allows the eyes of our understanding to see Jesus through a number of "pictures" in the Old Testament. Whereas the Western world majors in abstract thought, I expect this book to find special appeal with us here in Africa where picture language is the way of communication. This book should be put into the hands of those who need to hear the gospel afresh in this simple picture form. I cannot commend it too highly!'
CONRAD MBEWE, PASTOR OF KABWATA BAPTIST CHURCH, LUSAKA, ZAMBIA

'Kurt Strassner's *Hints and Signs of the Coming King* provides an attractive guidebook to help us discover for ourselves how the Old Testament points to Jesus. What's more, you can read it, enjoy it, and learn life-long principles for your own Bible study—all in about the same length of time as a walk from Jerusalem to Emmaus. Enjoy the journey!'
SINCLAIR B FERGUSON, SENIOR MINISTER, FIRST PRESBYTERIAN CHURCH, COLUMBIA, SOUTH CAROLINA

Pathways to peace

Facing the future with faith—
Meditations from Isaiah 40

JOHN KITCHEN

128PP, PAPERBACK

ISBN 978-1-84625-212-9

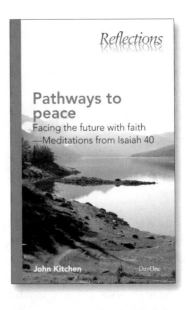

A million events assault the word tomorrow to make it the most uncertain word in the English language. As we stand at the threshold between a fretful past and a wishful future, what guarantee is there that tomorrow will be better than yesterday? Pathways to Peace sets forth the hope of Isaiah 40: Only God's presence sustains you in the panic of an uncertain future, and God's presence only helps you when you appreciate his preeminence over all things. Where God is lifted up as preeminent, he manifests his presence and the peace of God is the result in the believer's life..

'John Kitchen's book on Isaiah 40 is a joy to read with its strong encouragement on how the preeminence and presence of our Lord affects all we do, think, and hope for as believers. I strongly encourage a wide usage of this book among all who need a spiritual uplift in these troubling days.'
WALTER C. KAISER, JR., PRESIDENT EMERITUS, GORDON-CONWELL THEOLOGICAL SEMINARY

'This is a refreshing and health-giving meditation on the grandest of all themes: the nature of God and how it affects our living today. It will strengthen your spiritual muscles and equip you to face the challenges you encounter victoriously.'
AJITH FERNANDO, NATIONAL DIRECTOR, YOUTH FOR CHRIST, SRI LANKA

On wings of prayer
Praying the ACTS way

REGGIE WEEMS

112PP, PAPERBACK

ISBN 978-1-84625-178-8

Constructing a prayer life is often like putting a puzzle together without the box's cover. Having a picture makes all the difference. Bible prayers create a model of what prayer can be; exciting, fulfilling and powerful. Using a simple acrostic makes prayer memorable, interesting and focused. You too can learn to pray following this simple outline utilized by men and women who experience the transforming power of prayer.

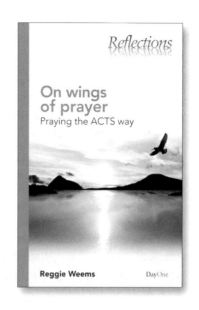

'This brief work on prayer will encourage you to pray, teach you to pray, and give you precious gems about prayer along the way. It taught me things I did not know, and reminded me of things I had forgotten.'
PAUL DAVID WASHER, HEARTCRY MISSIONARY SOCIETY

'Because of the unique nature of the Christian discipline of prayer, most books on prayer are more inspiring than they are helpful. Pastor Reggie Weems has achieved what only a few have ever done in Christian history. This book is orthodox, penetrating, motivating and inspiring, all in one slender, readable volume. If you are hoping to enhance your walk with the Master, here is one book that will bless your soul.'
PAIGE PATTERSON, PRESIDENT, SOUTHWESTERN BAPTIST THEOLOGICAL SEMINARY, FORT WORTH, TEXAS, USA

About Day One:

Day One's threefold commitment:
- To be faithful to the Bible, God's inerrant, infallible Word;
- To be relevant to our modern generation;
- To be excellent in our publication standards.

I continue to be thankful for the publications of Day One. They are biblical; they have sound theology; and they are relevant to the issues at hand. The material is condensed and manageable while, at the same time, being complete—a challenging balance to find. We are happy in our ministry to make use of these excellent publications.

JOHN MACARTHUR, PASTOR-TEACHER, GRACE COMMUNITY CHURCH, CALIFORNIA

It is a great encouragement to see Day One making such excellent progress. Their publications are always biblical, accessible and attractively produced, with no compromise on quality. Long may their progress continue and increase!

JOHN BLANCHARD, AUTHOR, EVANGELIST AND APOLOGIST

Visit our web site for more information and
to request a free catalogue of our books.

www.dayone.co.uk

U.S. web site:
www.dayonebookstore.com